Doris Olsen

Bobbin Lace Flowers

Akacia

Photography: P.E. Nikolajsen
Editor and Lay-out: I.L. Nikolajsen

3. edition
Printers: InPrint, Riga, 2012

ISBN: 978-87-7847-104-8

Preface

For a long time I have thought about how to make lace flowers, and achieve the look of "real flowers". One day the idea suddenly came to me, but it required a number of trials before I finally succeeded. However, once I got started the ideas kept coming and I could not work fast enough.

I showed a couple of my finished results to my lace friends and they were very impressed and they soon convinced me to present the flower patterns in a book.

It was quite a challenge to make so many flowers and therefore some of the 18 flowers in this book are inspired by real flowers and some have grown from my own fantasy.

The lace techniques used for the flowers are very simple. The essential technique is the use of a thin metal enamelled wire on the edges, which allows the petals and leaves to be formed into the desired shape.

I think that there is nothing more beautiful than a 3-dimensional lace flower and it is also a simple yet different beginner's lace, which has many possibilities. Try the orchid branch as a hat decoration or use them to decorate a dinner table, use a flower as a brooch, lay a flower in a tea-light stand or attach it to material and display it in a deep frame. There are many different alternatives.

The book contains explicit instructions with both working diagrams and prickings for all the flowers and also step by step guidance for assembling the parts and forming the "real" flower.

Begin by reading the useful hints at the start of the book and then you are ready to make your lace. Many of the techniques are obvious when actually making the lace.

Have fun, and I hope that you manage to produce a whole bouquet.

Doris Olsen

Lace Flowers

Photography: P.E. Nikolajsen
Editor and Lay-out: I.L. Nikolajsen

3. edition
Printers: InPrint, Riga, 2012

ISBN: 978-87-7847-104-8

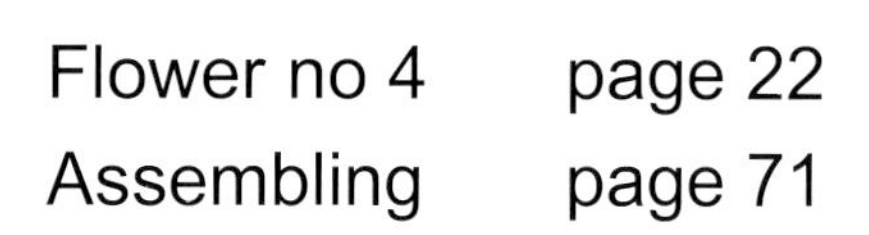

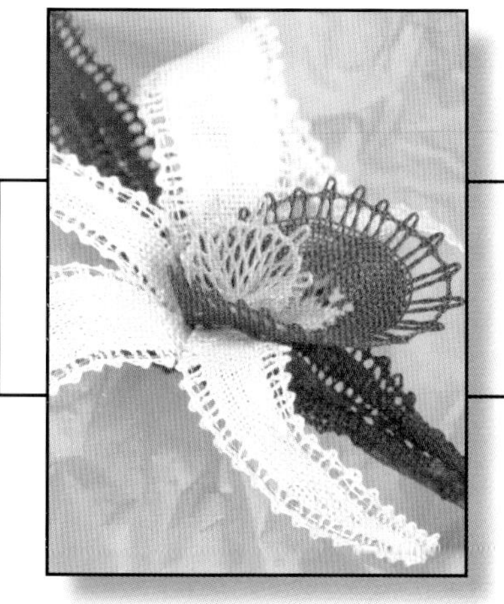

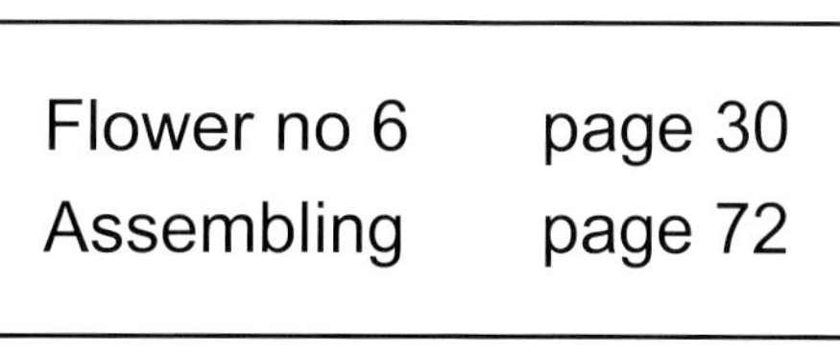

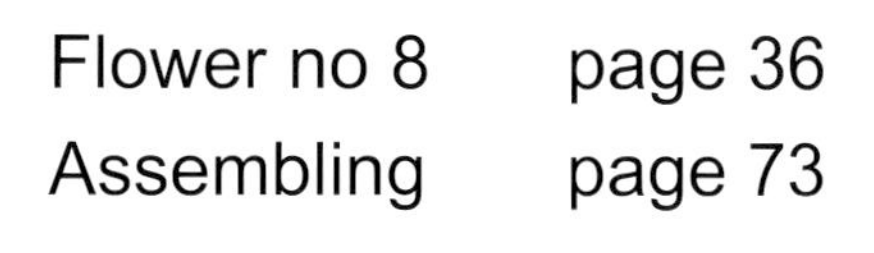

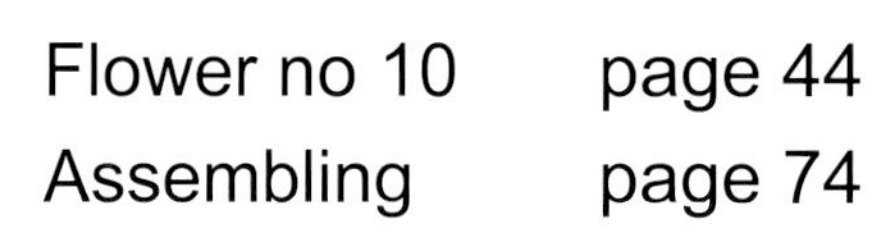

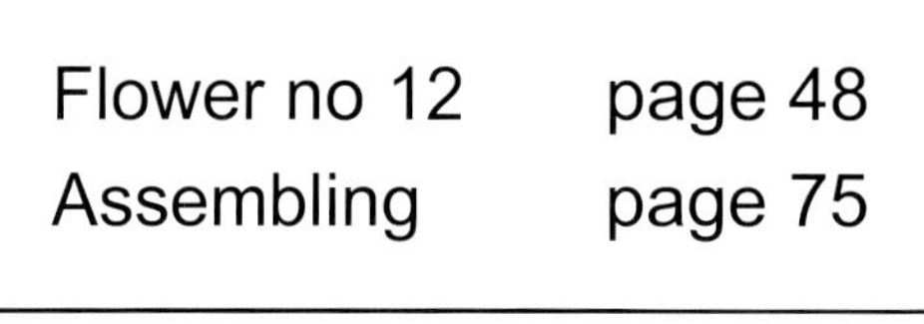

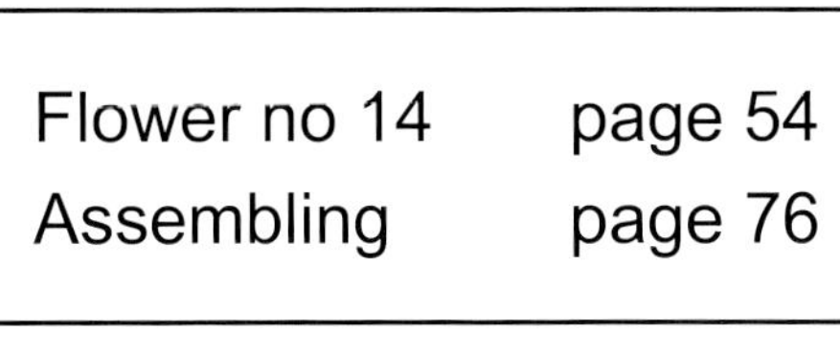

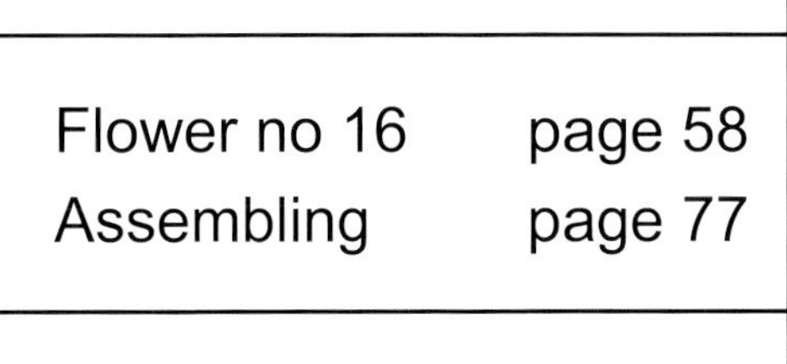

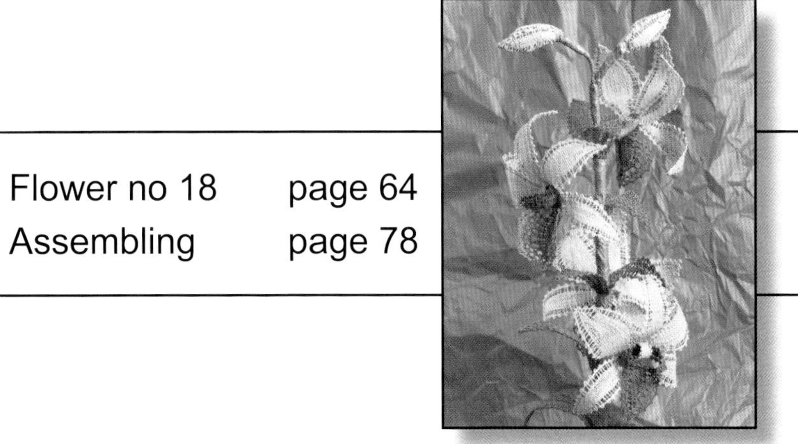

Materials

Thread and beads
The following threads are used for the flowers:
Cotton 80/3 from Anchor, DMC, Mayflower and Venus
Linen 80/3 from Goldschild

If a thread is unavailable, then substitute with DMC Mouliné 25, art. 117 in a wide selection of shades (use one of the 6 strands). See the thread comparison list page 79.

For added effect on certain flowers, use mini beads on the bobbin thread.

Enamelled wire
This is a soft metal wire found in various gauges and colours. The wire is mostly used by floral artists, but is becoming more and more common in lacemaking, because it is ideal as a gimp. It allows the finished lace to be shaped easily.
The thin 0.25mm enamelled wire is used for flowers and the 0.30mm matt green enamelled wire is use for leaves.
The gimp colour is chosen to match to the lace thread.
Leftover enamelled wire is used to assemble the flower.

Floral stub wire
Floral stub wire gauge 0.60mm is used for the flower stalks.

Floral tape
Green floral tape is used to cover the wire stalks.

Stamens

Stamens can be bought ready-made in different sizes. They can be matt white or in pearl-effect colours. The advantage of the matt white stamens is that they can be coloured with felt tip pens, hobby paint or ink to match the flower. The article number quoted in the pattern is the catalogue number of the supplier.

Stamens can also be made with beads on enamelled wire.

They can also be made of beads sewn into the flower centre.

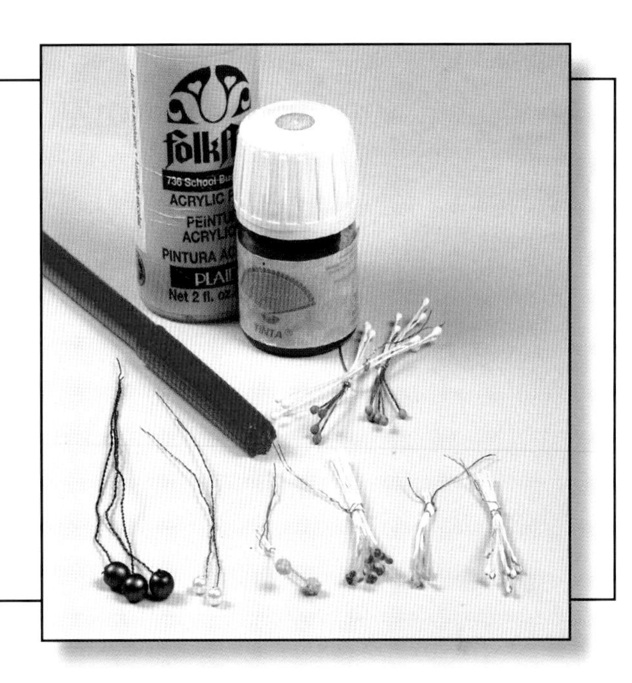

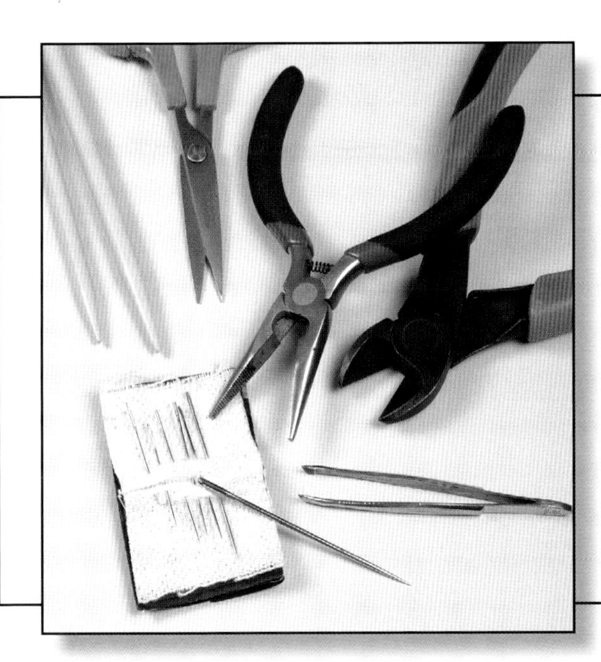

Tools for assembling

A good quality pair of wire cutters to cut the fine metal thread
A pair of narrow pliers to squeeze and twist the wire stalks
A pair of pointed scissors to trim off threads
A thick pointed darning needle to form holes in the finished and stiffened lace
A pair of fine tweezers to form petals and stamens
Knitting needles in a variety of gauges to form spirals
Sewing needle to stitch the parts together

Stiffener

The lace is stiffened with Belgian stiffener (from Kantcentrum, Bruges). The stiffener is applied undiluted with a paintbrush.

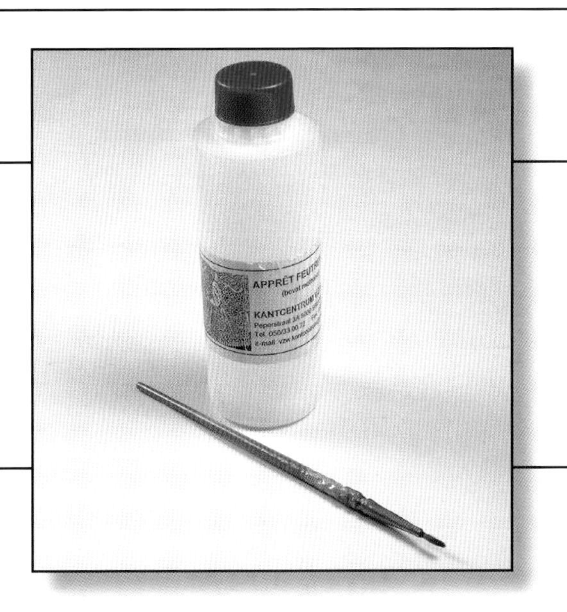

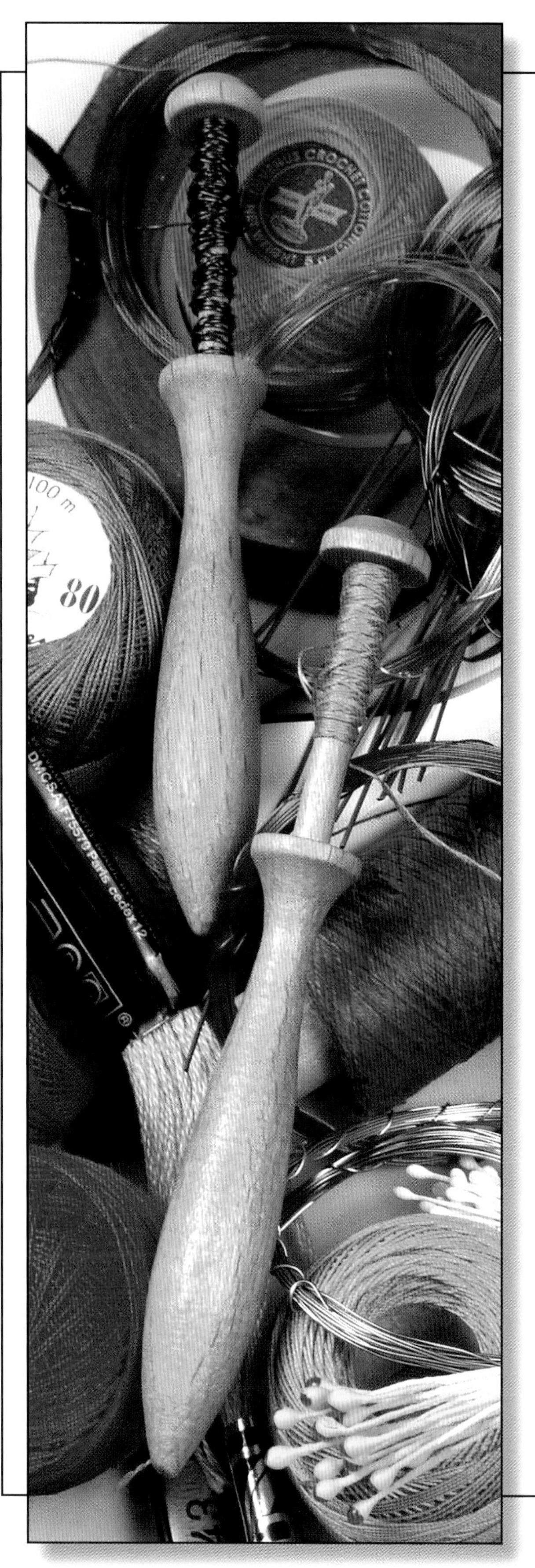

Before you begin

Only one pricking is provided for each part. However, it can be necessary to work up to 5 petals for the flower. It is a good idea to make several copies of the petal pricking in order to continue making another petal whilst the stiffener is drying on the previous petal.

It is necessary to stiffen twice before removing the lace from the pillow. It is very important to back the pricking with cardboard and cover it with plastic film.

Prick the holes on the pricking before making the lace, as this gives more accuracy.

All the threads are tied off in reef knots. Leave 3-5cm in excess when trimming. The threads can be twisted into the stalk. The threads can also be trimmed off completely.

The enamelled wire is always positioned as a gimp inside the edge pair.

Roll the entire 3-5metres of enamelled wire on to a bobbin and use directly if only one bobbin is required. If two bobbins are required, then roll the necessary amount on to the second bobbin. To avoid waste, the length required corresponds to the outline of the pricking.

When finishing off the enamelled wire it is twisted together several times and this avoids wrinkling the lace during the assembly of the flower.

Leave 4cm in excess when trimming the enamelled wire.

Remember to save the leftovers for assembling the flower.

Techniques

Add a pair in linen stitch

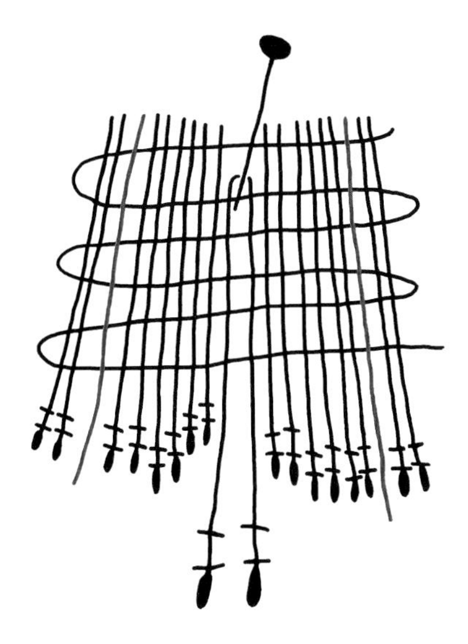

Remove a pair in linen stitch

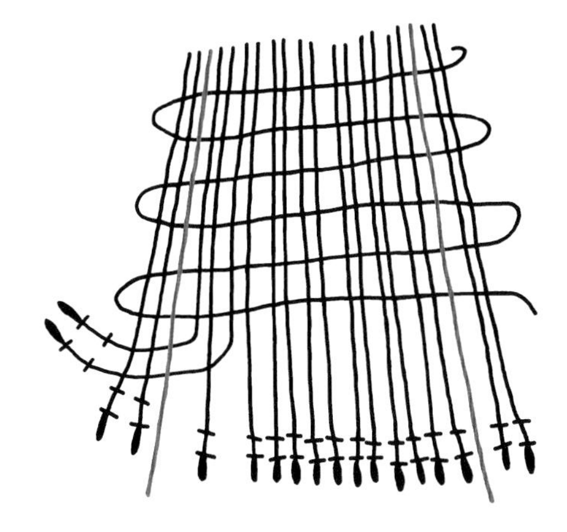

Counting from the gimp, bobbin 1 and 3 are laid aside. After completing the lace but before stiffening, the pairs are laid back into position.

Add a pair in half stitch

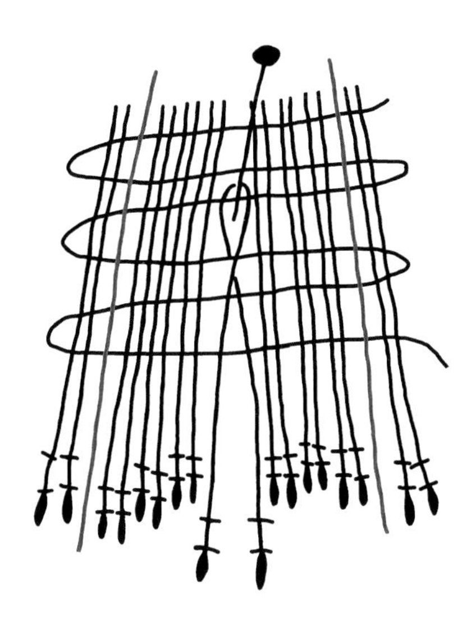

Remove a pair in half stitch

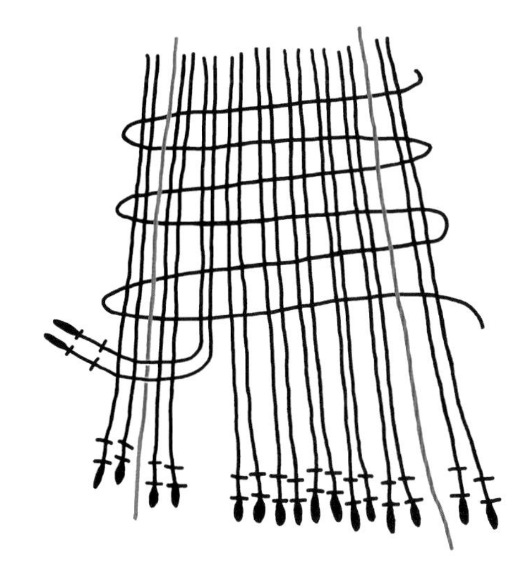

Counting from the gimp, bobbin 3 and 4 are laid aside. After completing the lace but before stiffening, the pairs are laid back into position.

Finishing off the enamelled wire

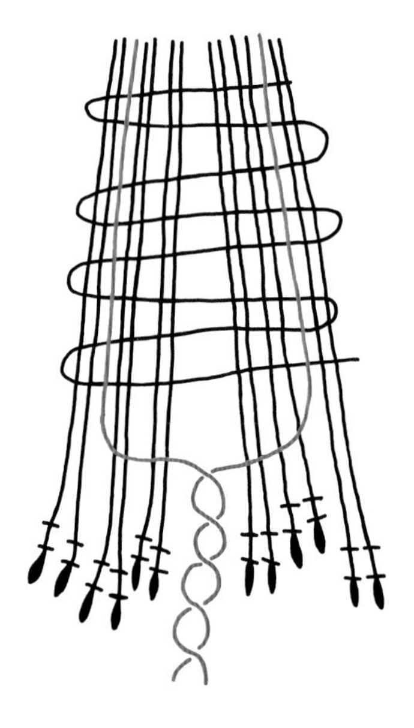

Twist the threads 4-5 times otherwise wrinkles can form when assembling the lace.

Plait with 2 pairs

Twist and cross throughout the plait.

Tally

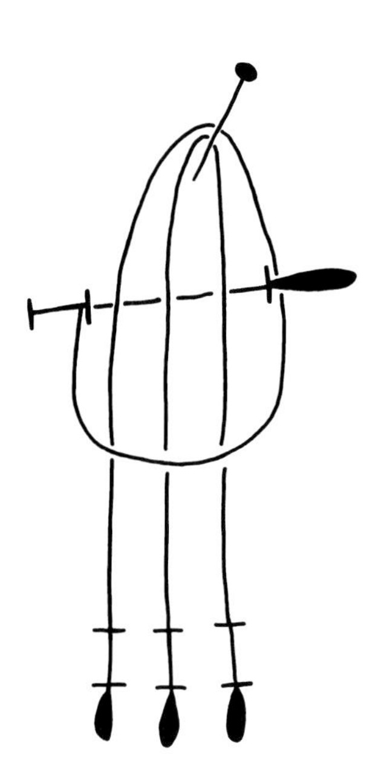

Step 1
Work with 2 pairs. Bobbin no 4 makes a half hitch over the other 3 bobbins.

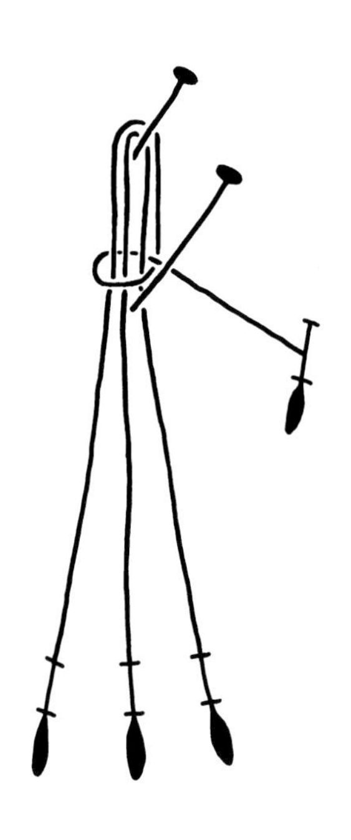

Step 2
Pull up the thread firmly

Step 3
Weave the tally with bobbin no 4 and use it also to secure the completed leaf with a half hitch as in step 1.

Turn stitch

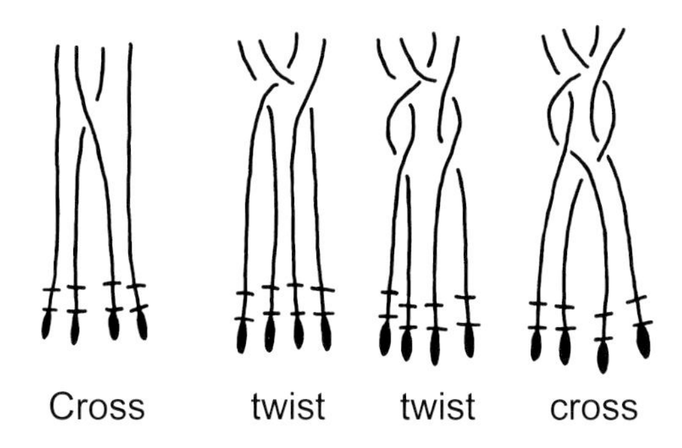

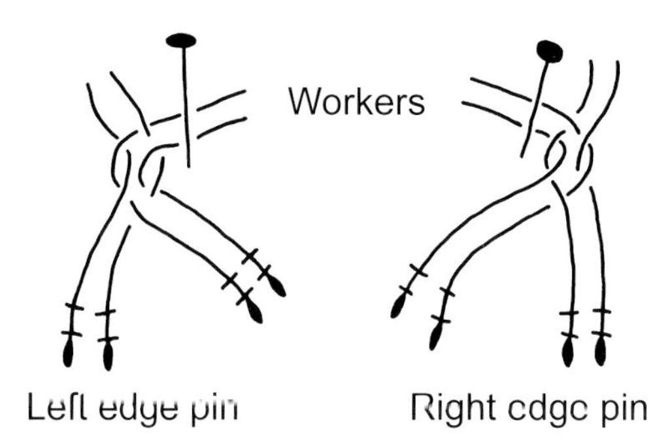

Reef knot finish

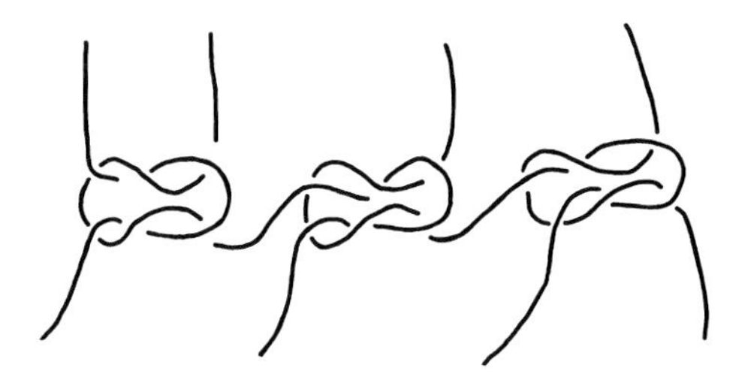

Start at the left and tie the first pair in a reef knot. Lay the left bobbin aside and take the next bobbin to the right for the next reef knot. Continue in this way until all the bobbins are tied off.

Codes and Symbols

Symbols

= Linen stitch

= Half stitch

= Whole stitch on working diagrams

= Enamelled wire on working diagrams
Also twists – pins – leaves

= Enamelled wire on technique diagrams

= Turn stitch

= Sewing

= Plait

Pricking
– full size

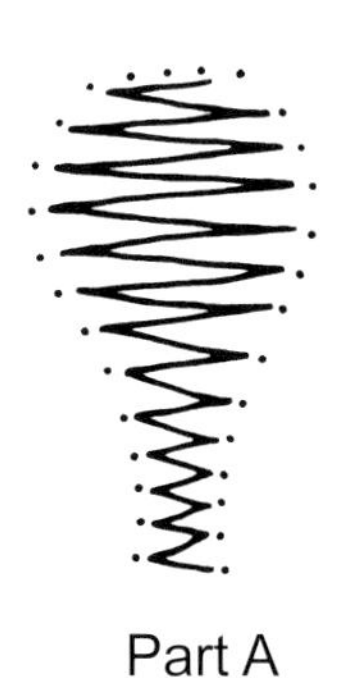

Part A

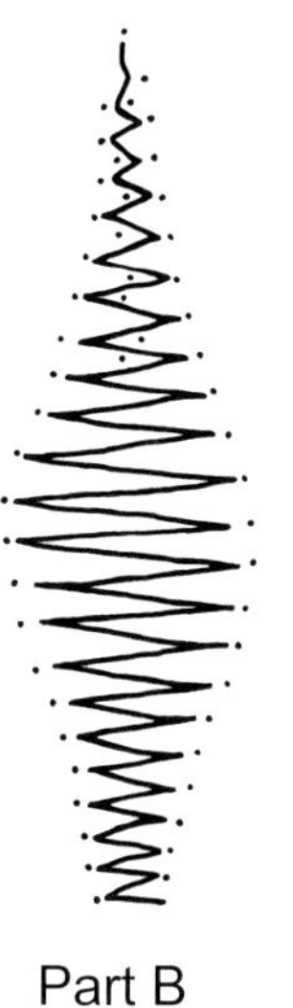

Part B

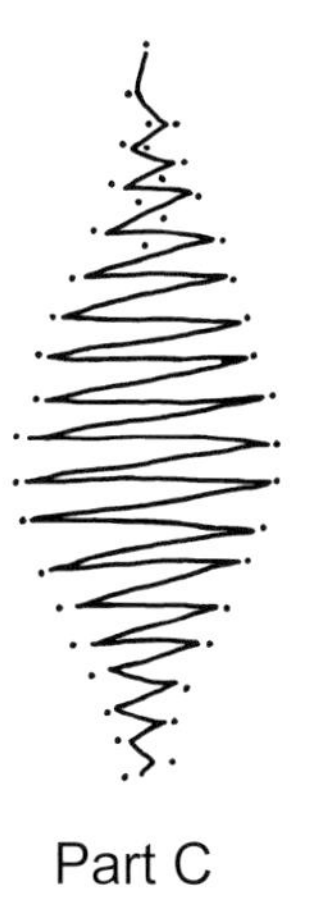

Part C

Thread
Anchor col 46, red
DMC col 210, light lilac
Goldschild col 41, hunting green

Enamelled wire
Wire 0.25mm, red and lilac

Pairs
See text

Assembling – see page 68
Floral stub wire 0.60mm
Floral tape
Stamens no S.06

Part A
Inner petals, 4 pieces
Work in half stitch with a whole stitch edge.
8 pairs lilac + 1 pair lilac Wire.
Remove pairs as indicated in the diagram.

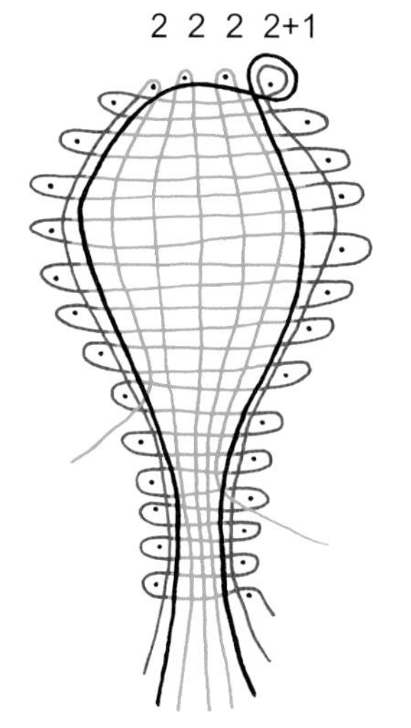

Part B
Outer petals, 4 pieces
Work in linen stitch
Begin with 3 pairs red + 1 pair red Wire.
Add pairs (altogether 11) and remove as indicated.

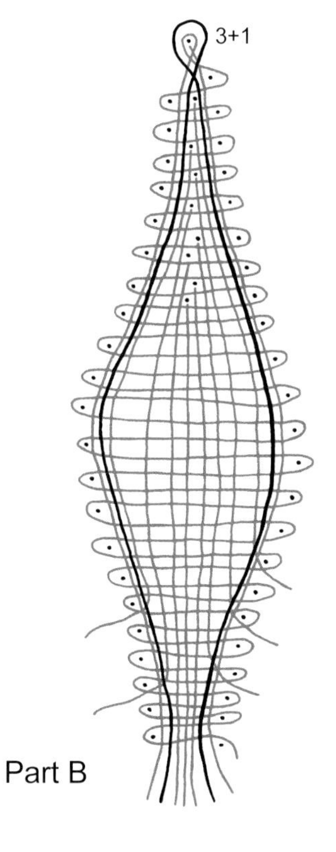

Part B

Part C
Leaf, 2 pieces.
Work in linen stitch with twists as indicated.
Start with 3 pairs hunting green.
Add pairs (altogether 9) and remove as indicated.

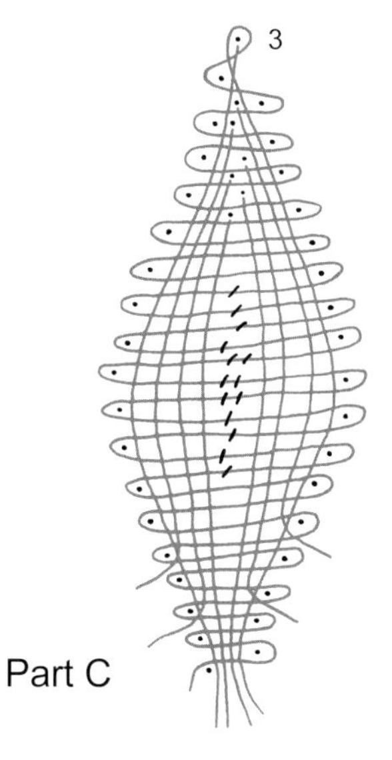

Part C

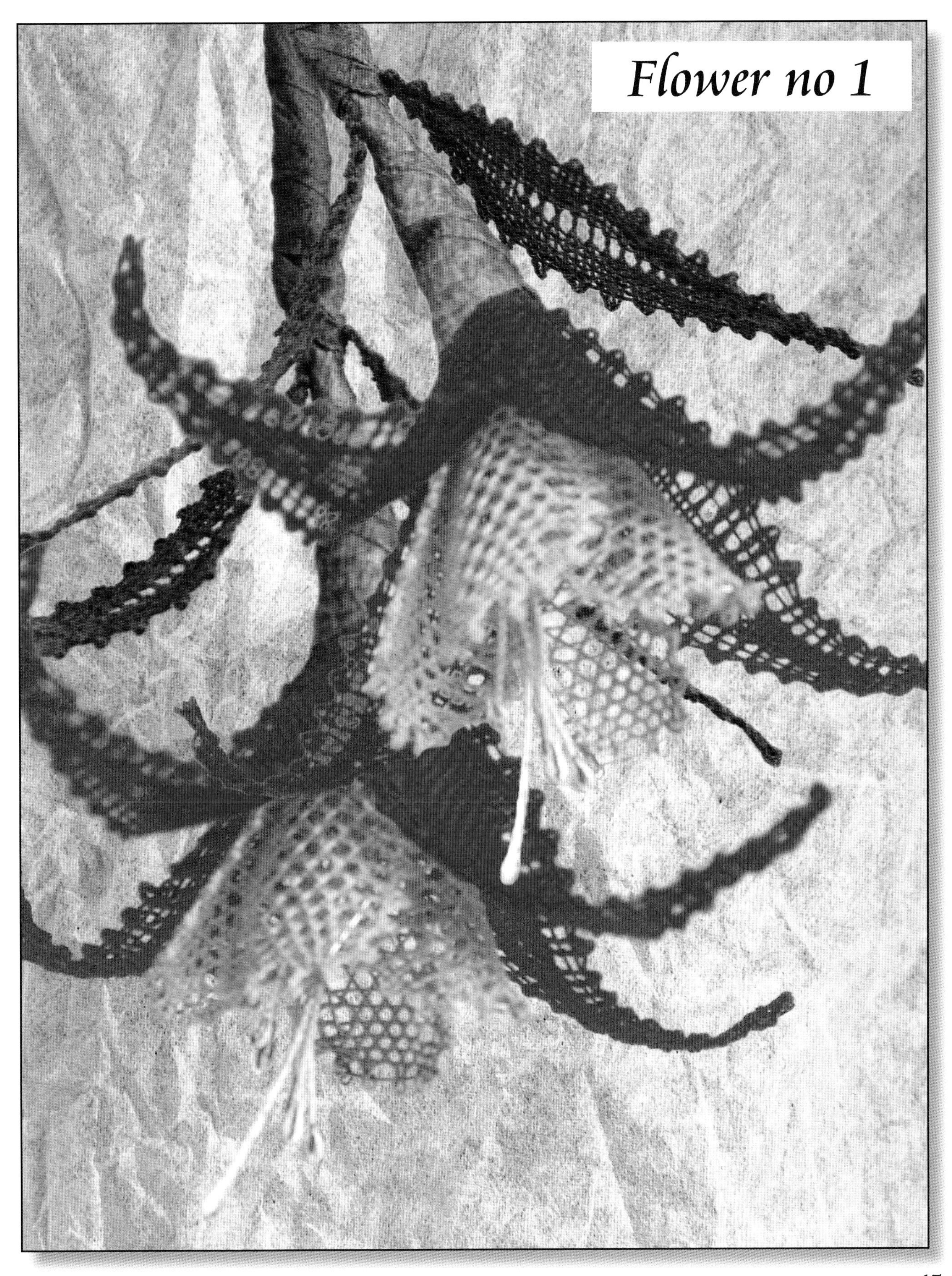

Flower no 1

Thread
DMC col 666, red
Goldschild col 41, hunting green

Enamelled wire
Wire 0.25mm, red
Wire 0.30mm, matt green

Pairs
See text

Assembling – see page 70
Floral stub wire 0.60mm
Floral tape
Stamens no S.22
Hobby paint, yellow and red.

Part A
Largest petals, 1 piece.
Work in linen stitch with whole stitch on the outer and inner edge.
7 pairs red + 1 bobbin red wire.
Make sewings in the middle.
Join the start to the finish and tie off with reef knots.

Part B
Petals, 1 piece
Work in half stitch with whole stitch on the inner and outer edges.
6 pairs red + 1 bobbin red wire.

Part C
Petals, 1 piece.
Work as for part B
5 pairs red + 1 bobbin red wire.

Part D
Smaller petals, 1 piece.
Work as for part B.
4 pairs red + 1 bobbin red wire.

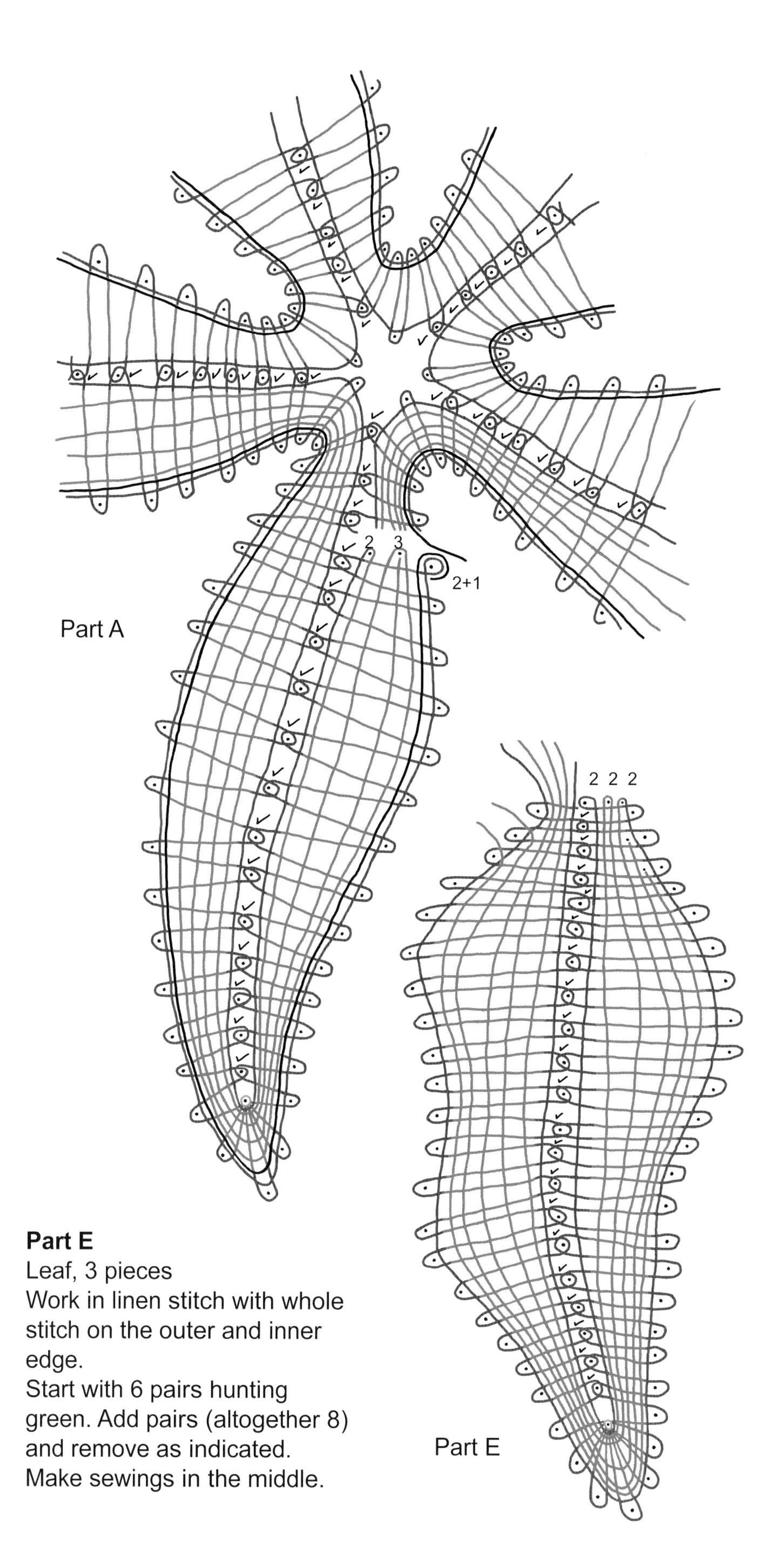

Part E
Leaf, 3 pieces
Work in linen stitch with whole stitch on the outer and inner edge.
Start with 6 pairs hunting green. Add pairs (altogether 8) and remove as indicated.
Make sewings in the middle.

Flower no 2

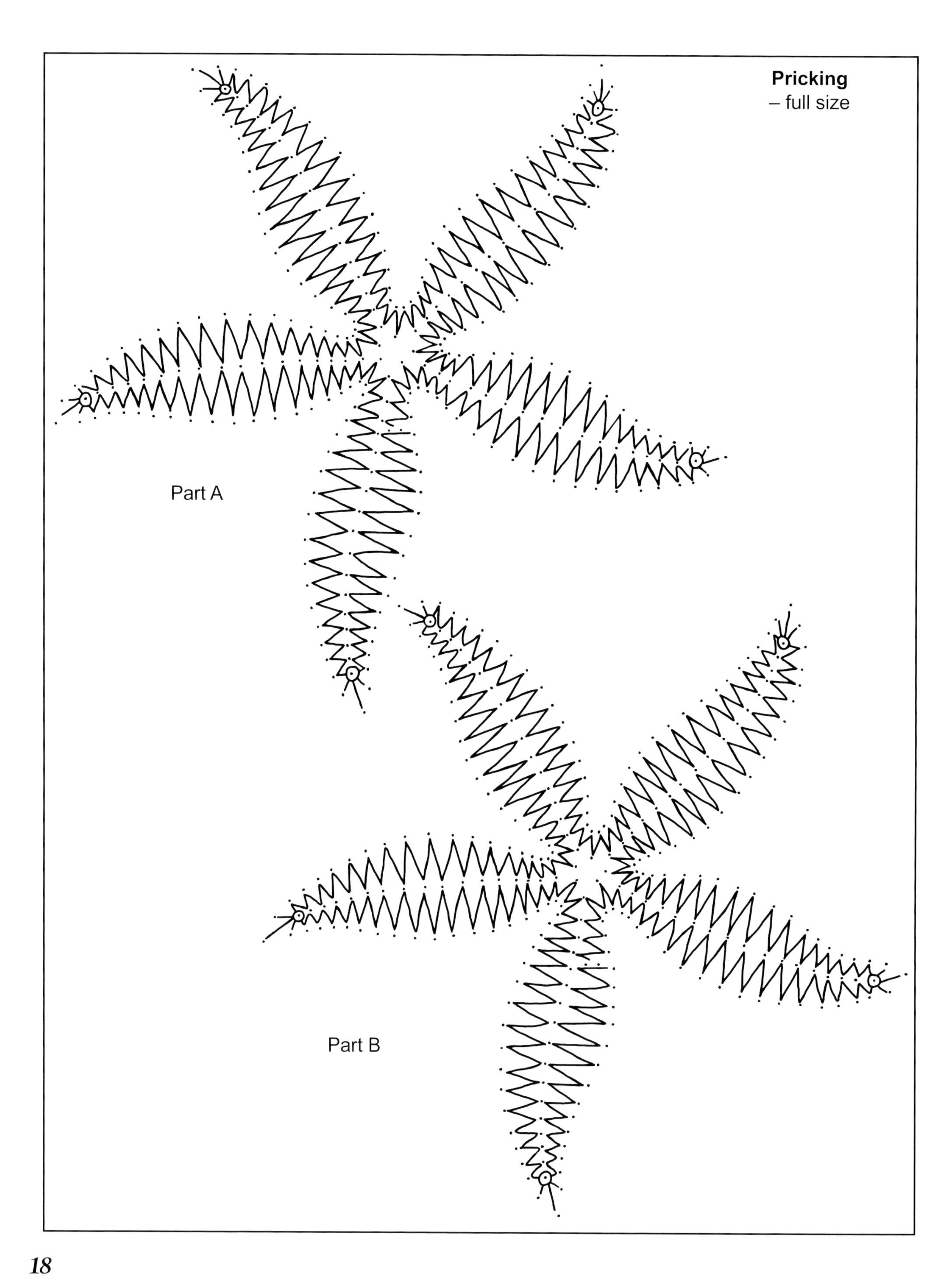
Pricking
– full size
Part A
Part B

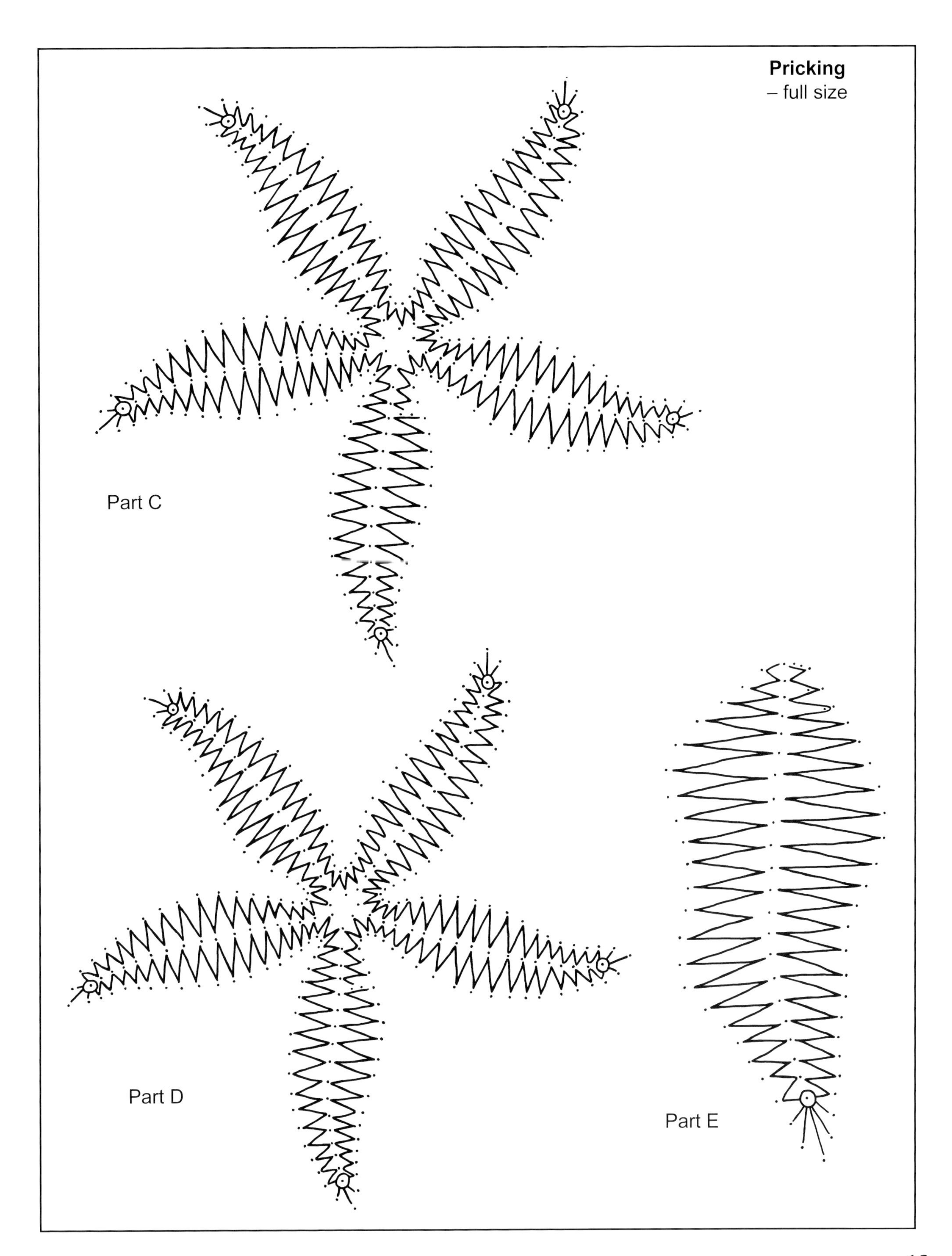
Pricking
– full size
Part C
Part D
Part E

Pricking
– full size

Part A

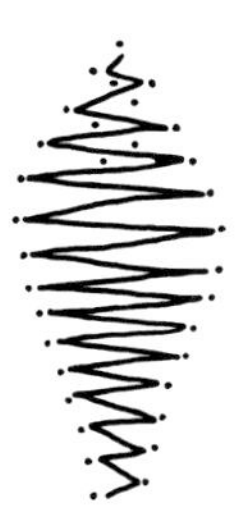

Part B

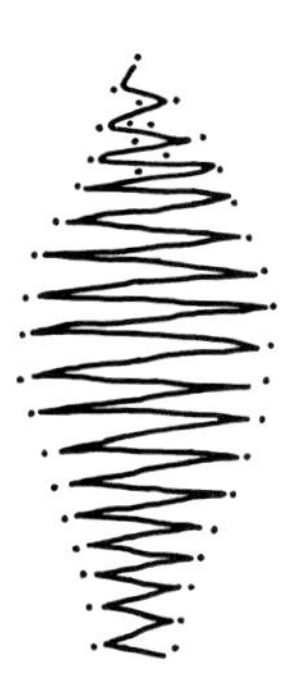

Part C

Thread
Anchor col 249, yellow
Mayflower col 1120, orange
Mayflower col 5520, light green

Enamelled wire
Wire 0.25mm, May green and also gold.

Pairs
See text

Assembling – see page 70
Floral stub wire 0.60mm
Floral tape
Stamens no S.16
Hobby paint, yellow

Part A
Petal, 5 pieces
Work in linen stitch.
Start with 3 pairs yellow + 1 pair gold wire.
Add pairs (altogether 11) and remove as indicated.
At x lay the yellow workers aside and add 1 orange pai

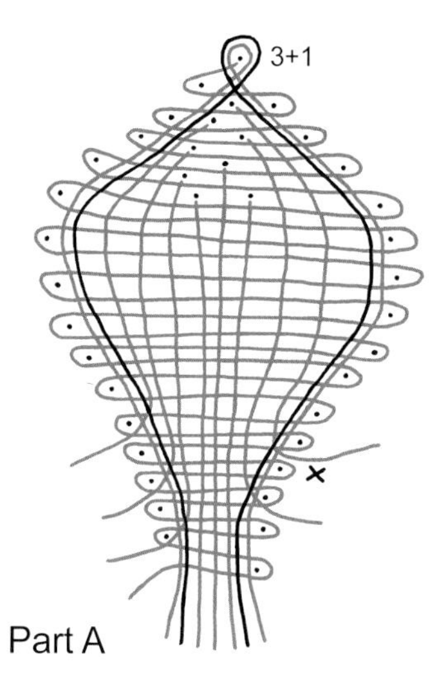

Part A

Part B
Bud petal, 3 pieces.
Work in linen stitch.
Start with 3 pairs yellow + 1 pair gold wire.
Add pairs (altogether 8) and remove as indicated.
At x lay the yellow workers aside and add 1 orange pair.

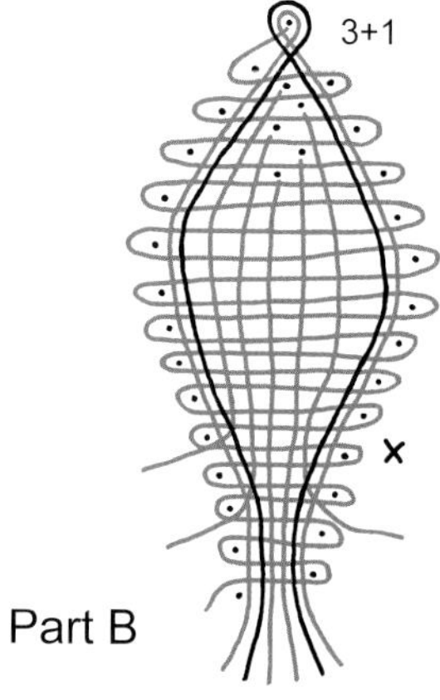

Part B

Part C
Leaf, 3 pieces
Work in linen stitch with twists as indicated.
Start with 3 pairs light green + 1 pair May green wire.
Add pairs (altogether 9) and remove as indicated.

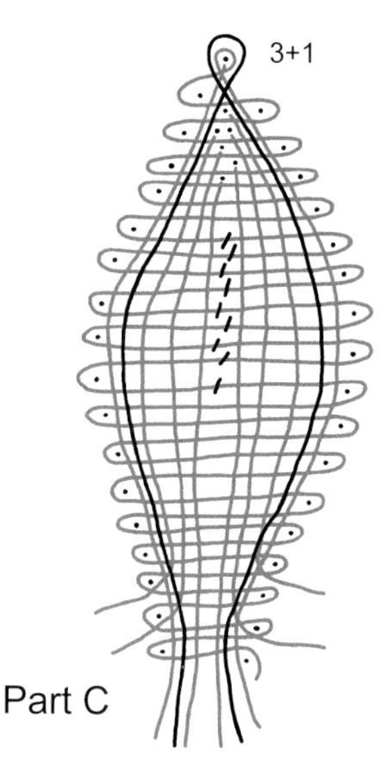

Part C

Flower no 3

Thread
DMC col 3688, dusty red

Enamelled wire
Wire 0.25mm, wine red

Pairs
See text

&
Mini beads 1.5mm, col 502, wine red

Assembly - see page 71.
Floral stub wire 0.60mm
Floral tape

Part A
Outer petals, 1 piece.
Work in half stitch with whole stitch on the outer and inner edge.
Start with 5 pairs dusty red + 1 bobbin wine red wire.
Use support pins at the points of the petals to hold the wire in position.
Join the start to the finish and tie off in reef knots.

Part B
Inner petals, I piece.
Work as part for A with 5 pairs of dusty red + 1 bobbin of wine red wire.
Thread 10 – 12 beads on each pair, positioning the beads randomly throughout the lace.
It is not necessary to use all the beads, but it is best with an excess of beads because the threads change constantly in half stitch.

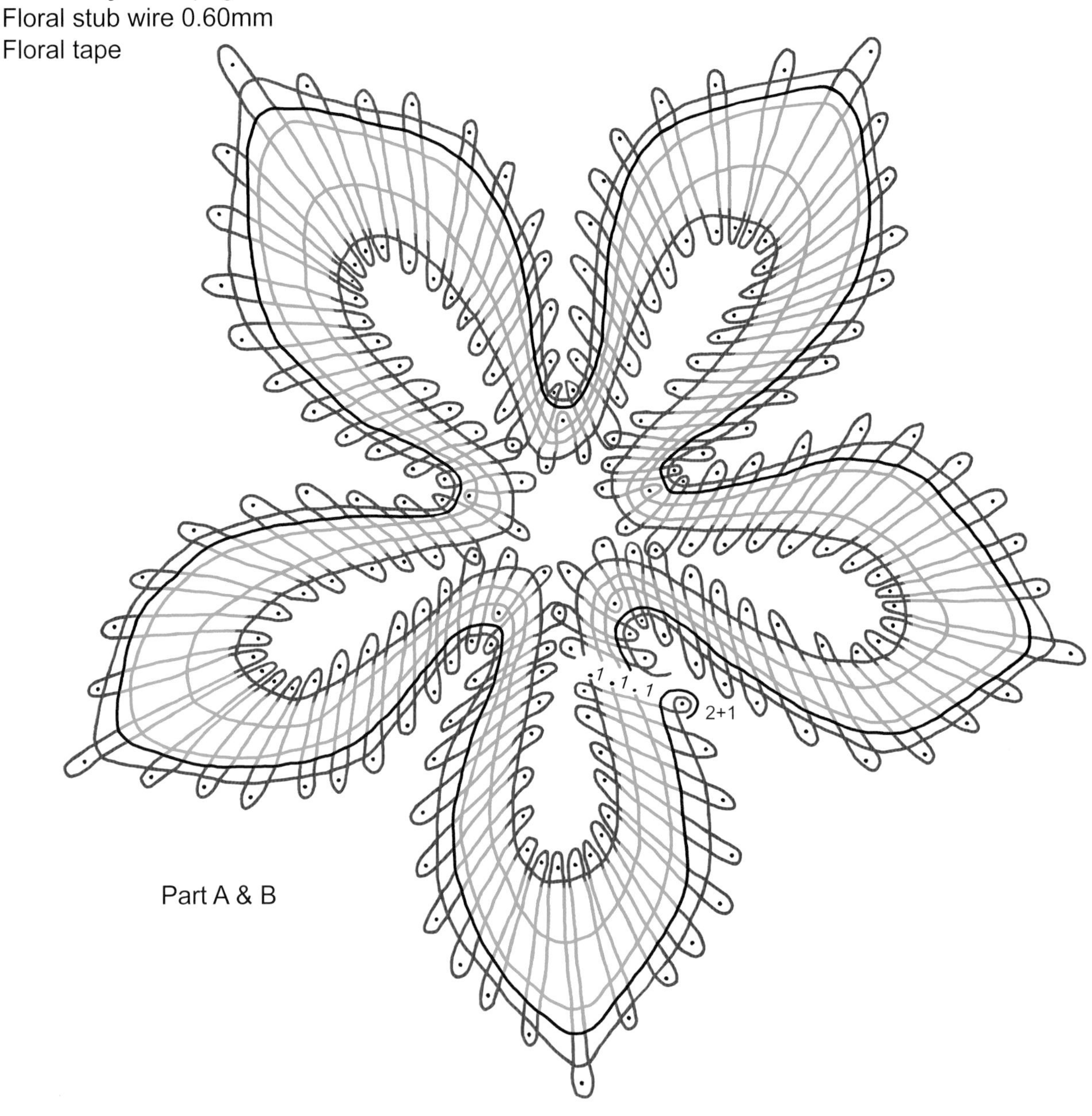

Part A & B

Flower no 4

Part C
Spiral, 3 pieces
Work in linen stitch
Start with 3 pairs dusty red + 1 pair wine red wire.
Thread 8–10 beads on the workers.
Position the 6 pairs as shown.

Part D
Centre rosette, 1 piece
Work in half stitch with whole stitch at both edges. Use 6 pairs dusty red.

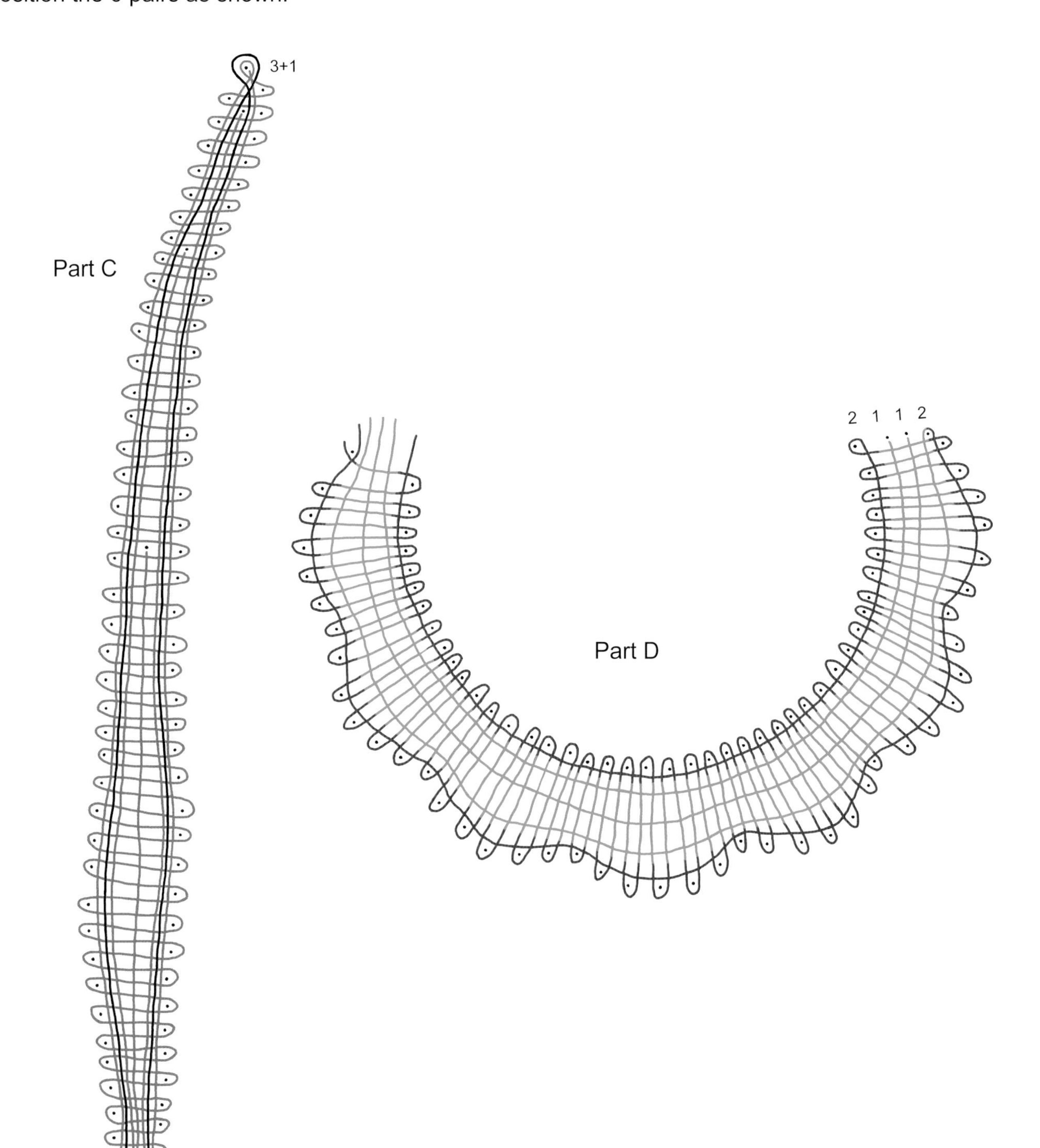

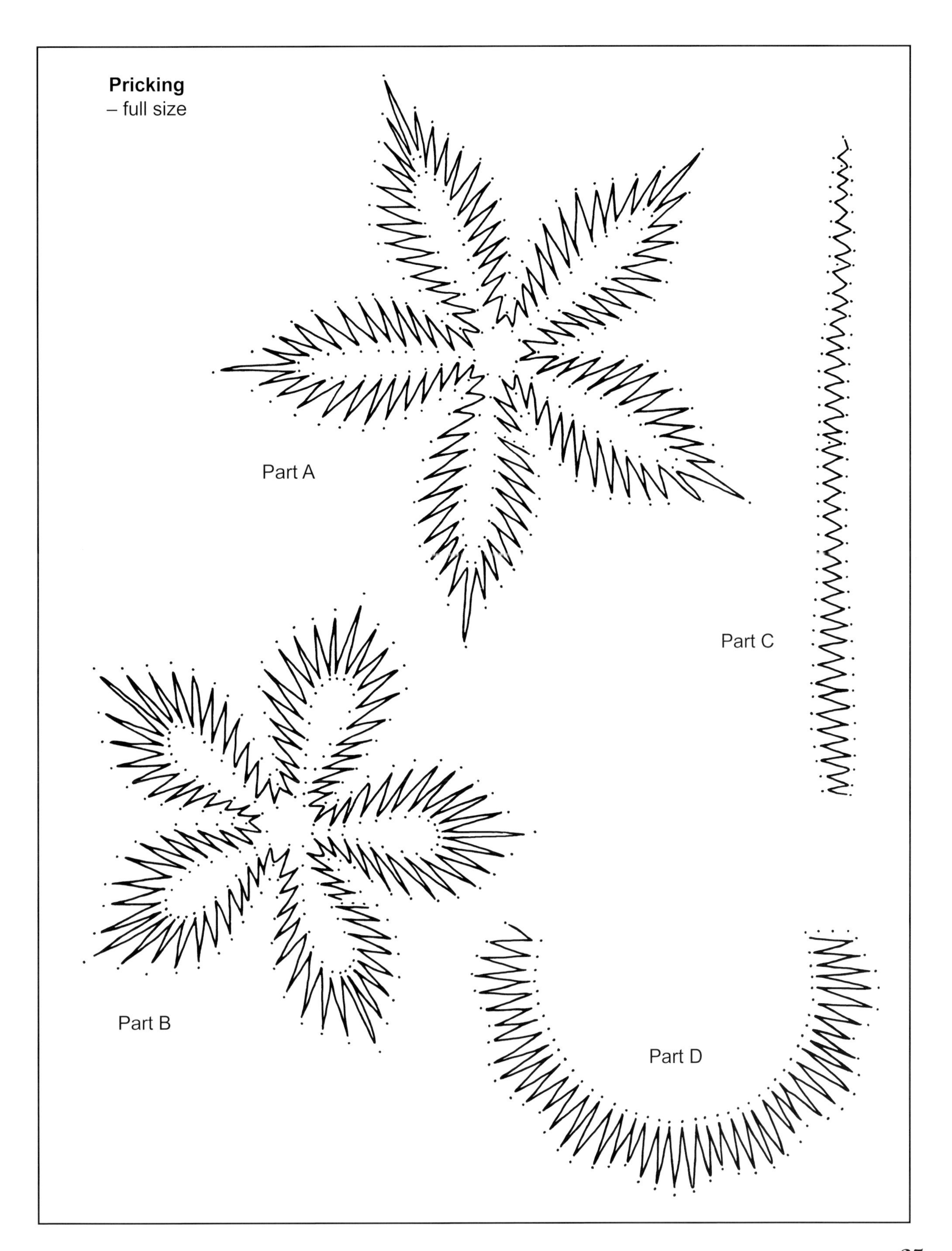
Pricking
– full size
Part A
Part C
Part B
Part D

Thread
DMC col B5200, white
Anchor col 249, yellow
DMC col 917 red/purple
Goldschild col 41, hunting green

Enamelled wire
Wire 0.25mm, silver

Pairs
See text

Assembly – see page 71
Floral stub wire 0.60mm
Floral tape

Part A
Outer petals, 2 pieces
Work in linen stitch. Start with 3 pairs white + 1 pair silver wire. Add pairs (altogether 9) and remove as indicated.

Part B
Middle petals, 2 pieces
Work as for part A. Start with 4 pairs white + 1 pair silver wire. Add pairs (altogether 15) and remove as indicated.

Part C
Inner petals, 1 piece
Work as for part A. Start with 3 pairs white + 1 pair silver wire. Add pairs (altogether 10) and remove as indicated.

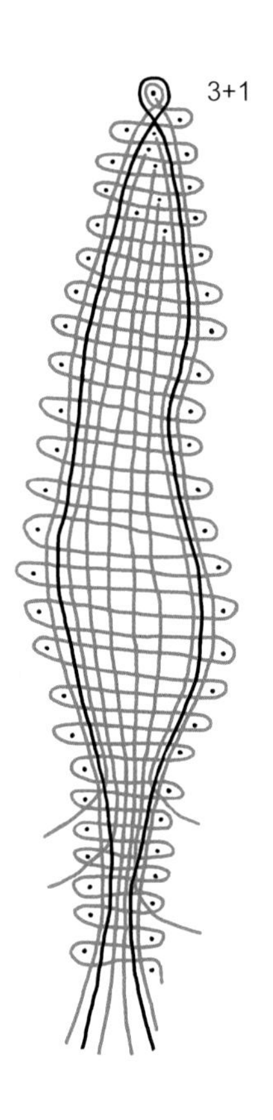

Part A

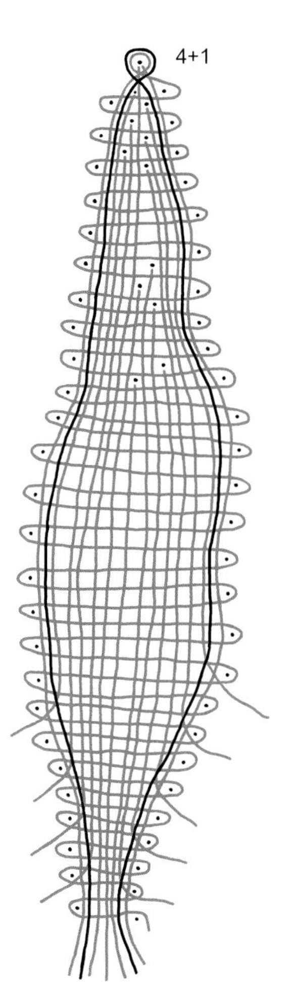

Part B

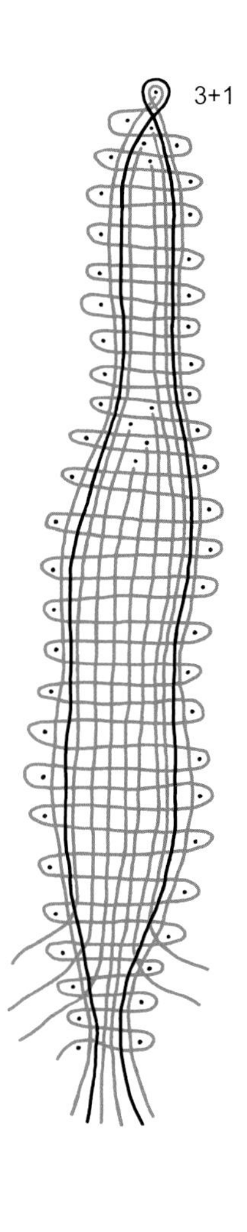

Part C

Flower no 5

Part D
Stamens, 1 piece
Work in half stitch with whole stitch on both edges, using 5 pairs yellow.

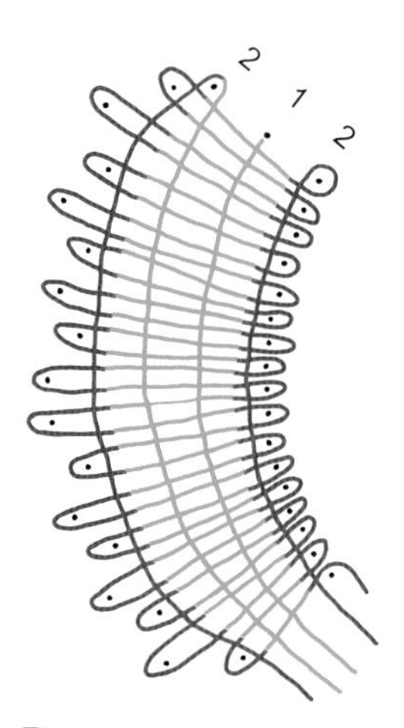

Part D

Part E
Lip, 1 piece
Work in linen stitch with twists on the outer edge. Start with the inner part using 7 pairs yellow. Work the outer border using 8 pairs red/purple and make sewings to the inner part.

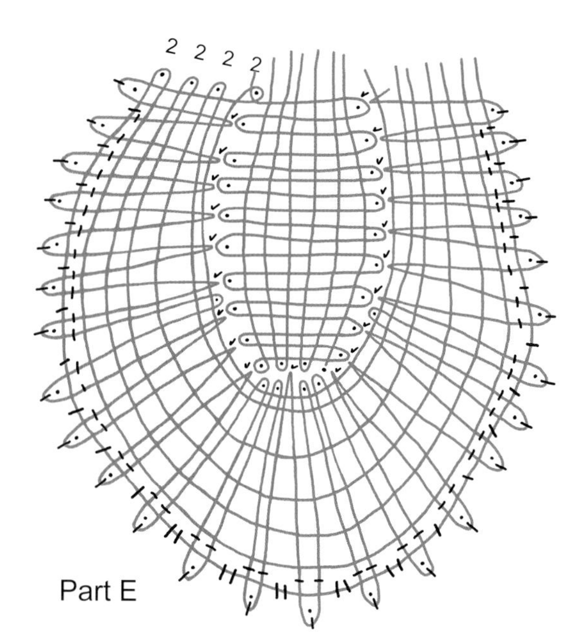

Part E

Part F and G
Leaf, 1 piece
Work in linen stitch with twists as indicated. Start with 3 pairs green and 1 pair wire. Add pairs (altogether 11) and remove as indicated.

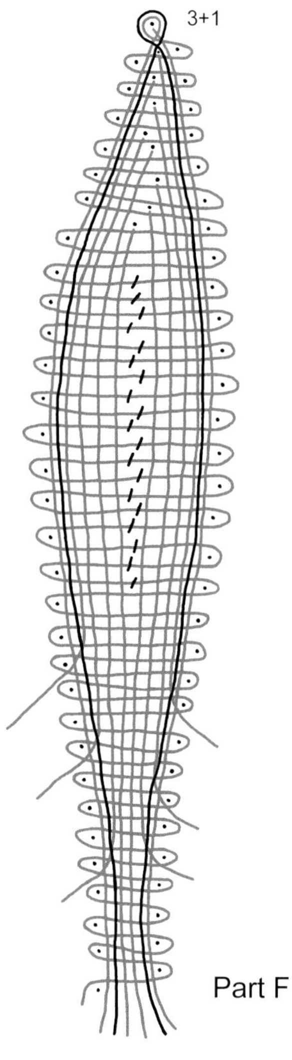

Part F

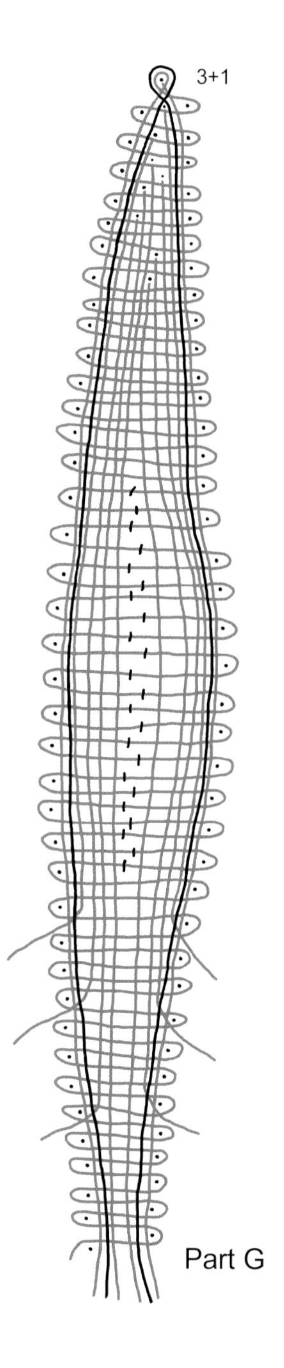

Part G

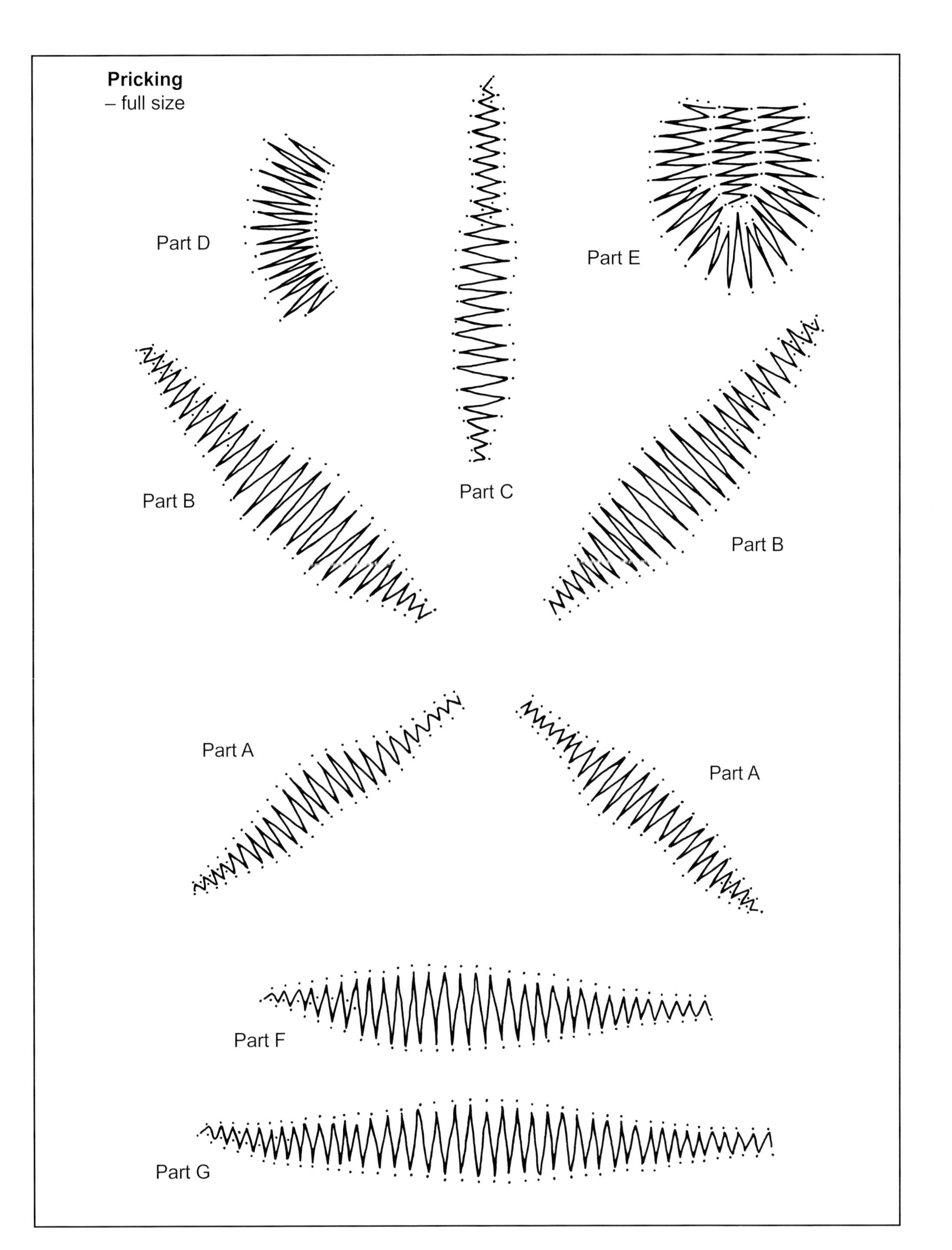
Pricking
– full size
Part D
Part E
Part B
Part C
Part B
Part A
Part A
Part F
Part G

Pricking
– full size

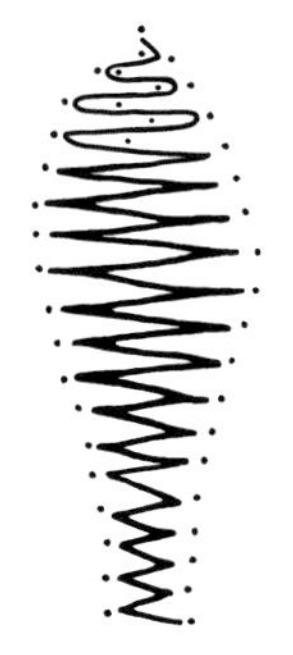

Part A

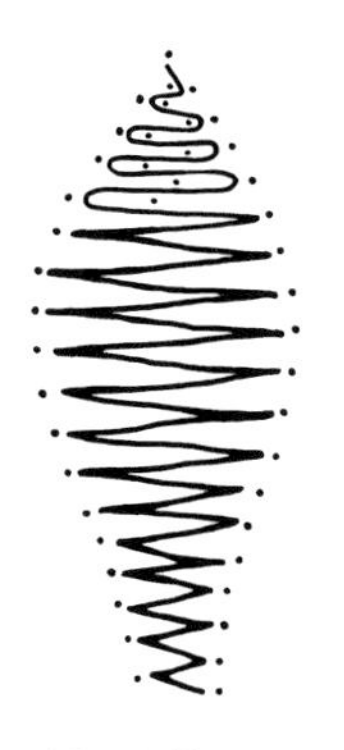

Part B

Part C

Thread
Anchor col 97, lilac
Mayflower col 2110, green
Leftover white thread

Enamelled wire
Wire 0.25mm, silver or light lilac
Wire 0.30mm, matt green

Pairs
See text

Assembling – see page 72
Floral stub wire 0.60mm
Floral tape
Stamens, no B.03
Hobby paint, yellow

Part A
Inner petals, 3 pieces
Work in linen stitch. Start with 3 pairs lilac + 1 pair wire. Add pairs (altogether 9) and remove as indicated.

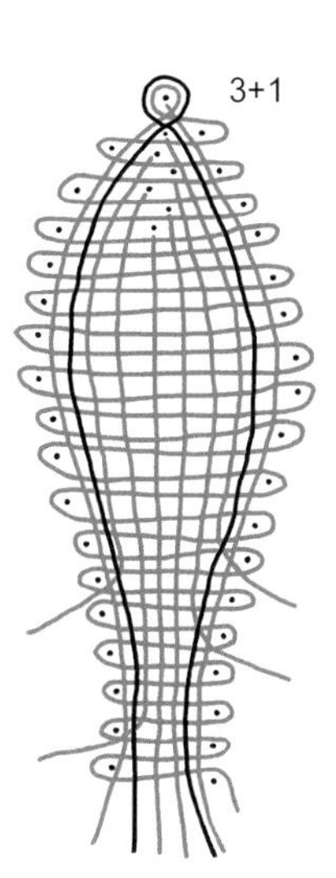

Part A

Part B
Outer petals, 3 pieces
Work as for part A. Add pairs (altogether 11) and remove as indicated.

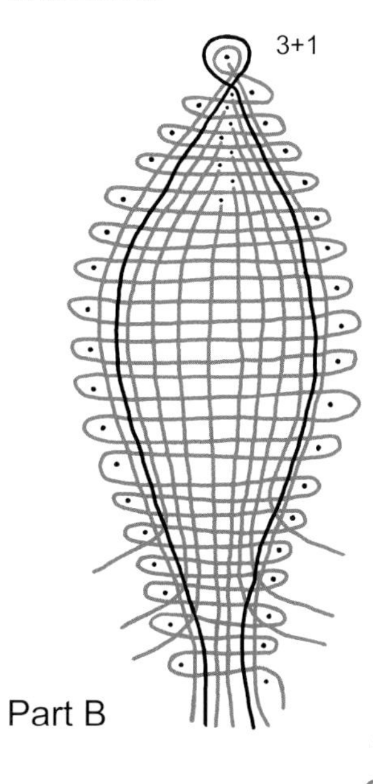

Part B

Part C
Leaf, 3 pieces
Work in linen stitch. Start with 5 pairs green + 1 pair green wire. Add 1 pair white in the middle and remove as indicated.

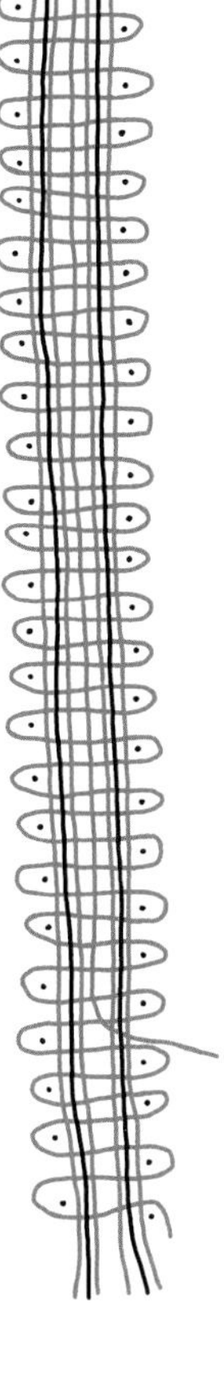

Part C

Flower no 6

Thread
Anchor col 259, light green
Mayflower col 5520, green
Anchor col 107, lilac

Enamelled wire
Wire 0.25mm May green

Pairs
See text

&
Clear beads, ca. 2mm

Assembling – see page 72
Floral stub wire 0.60mm
Floral tape

Part A
Inner petals, 6 pieces
Work in linen stitch with plaits in between, using 4 pairs lilac.

Part B
Large petals, 3 pieces
Work in linen stitch with twists as indicated. Start with 3 pairs light green. Add pairs (altogether 11) and remove as indicated.

Part C
Small petals, 3 pieces
Work in linen stitch with twists as indicated. Start with 3 pairs light green. Add pairs (altogether 9) and remove as indicated.

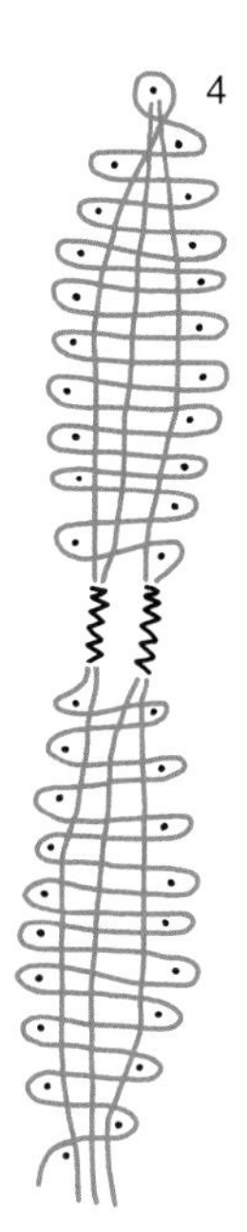

Part A

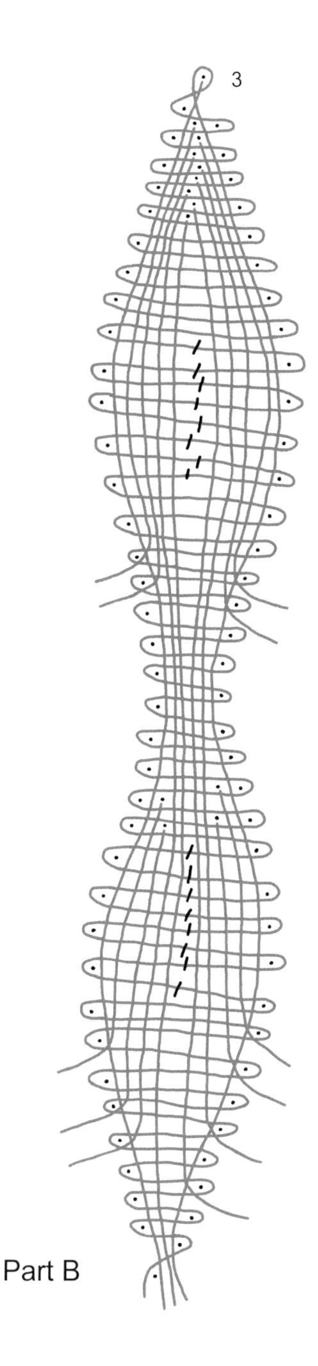

Part B

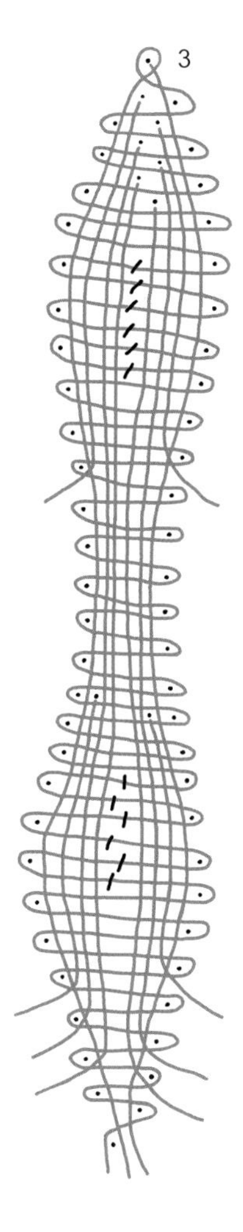

Part C

Flower no 7

Part D

Large leaf, 1 piece

Work in linen stitch with twists as indicated. Start with 4 pairs green + 1 pair May green wire. Add pairs (altogether 13) and remove as indicated.

Part E

Small leaf, 2 pieces

Work in linen stitch with twists as indicated. Start with 3 pairs green + 1 pair May green wire. Add pairs (altogether 11) and remove as indicated.

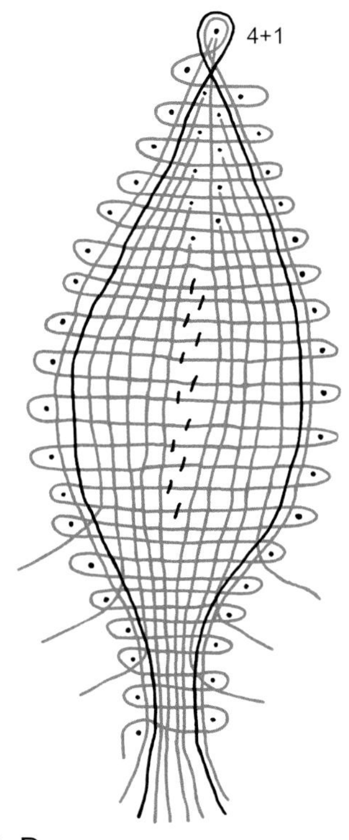

Part D

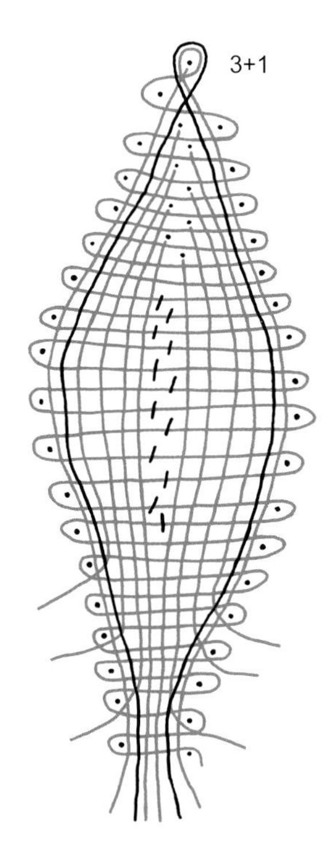

Part E

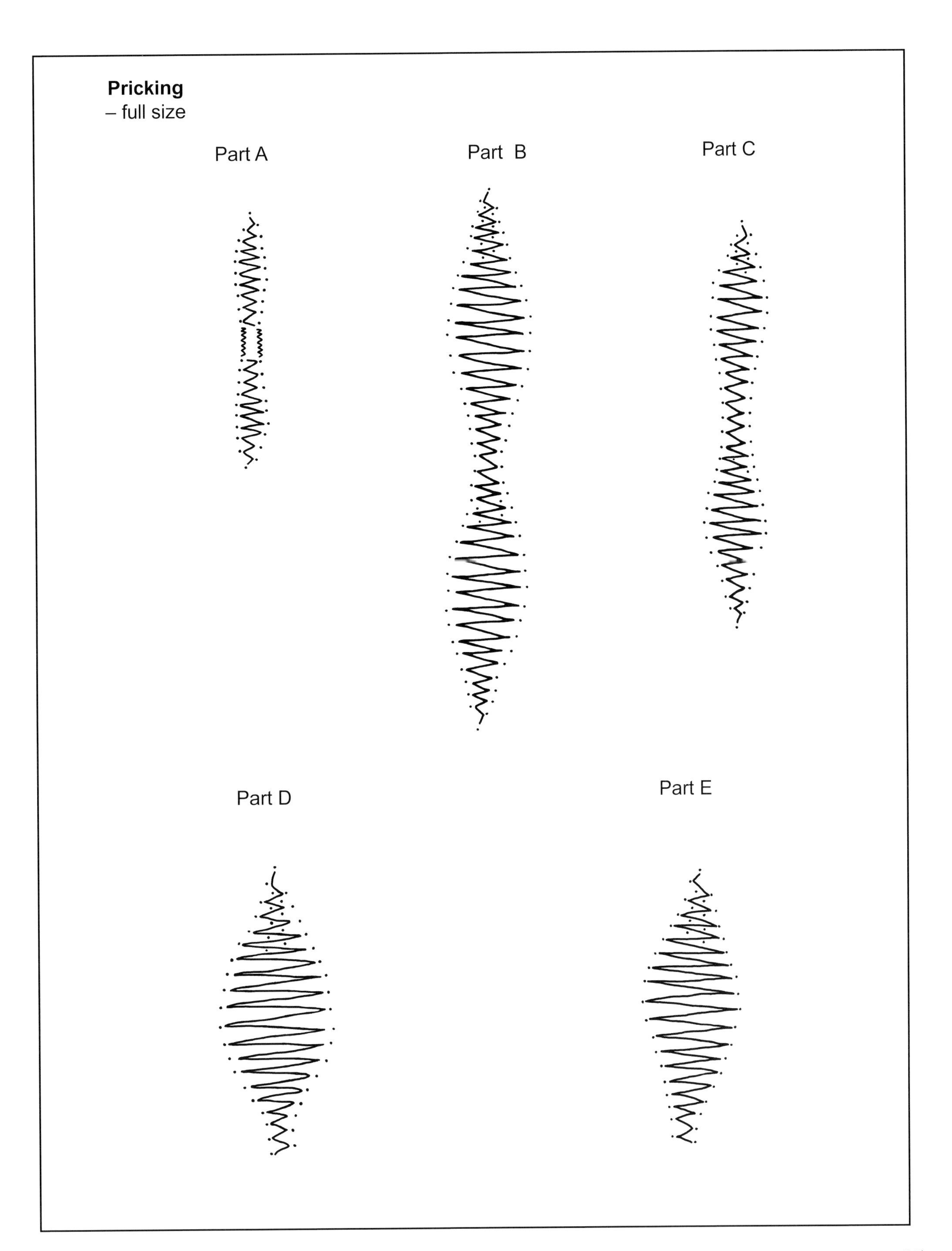
Pricking
– full size
Part A
Part B
Part C
Part D
Part E

Thread
DMC col 917, red/ lilac
DMC col 3608, light red
Mayflower col 1438, yellow
Goldschild col 41, hunting green
A leftover white thread

Enamelled wire
Wire 0.25mm, red/lilac
Wire 0.30mm, matt green

Pairs
See text

Assembling- see page 73
Floral stub wire 0.60mm
Floral tape

Part A
Upper petal, 1 piece
Work in linen stitch. Start with 3 pairs red/lilac + 1 pair red/lilac wire. Add pairs (altogether 9) and remove as indicated.

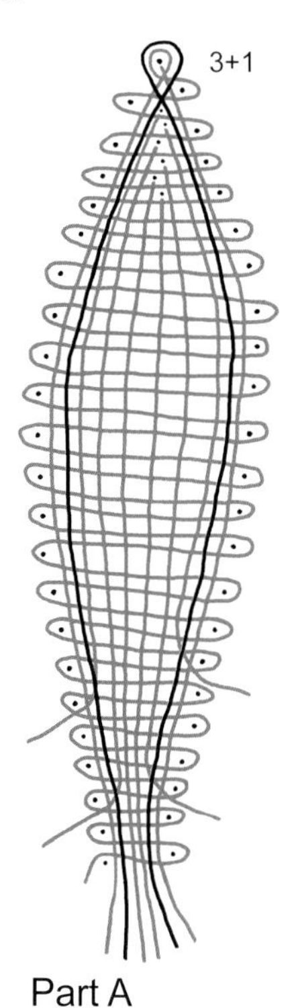

Part A

Part B
Lower petal, 2 pieces
Work as for part A. Add pairs (altogether 9) and remove as indicated.

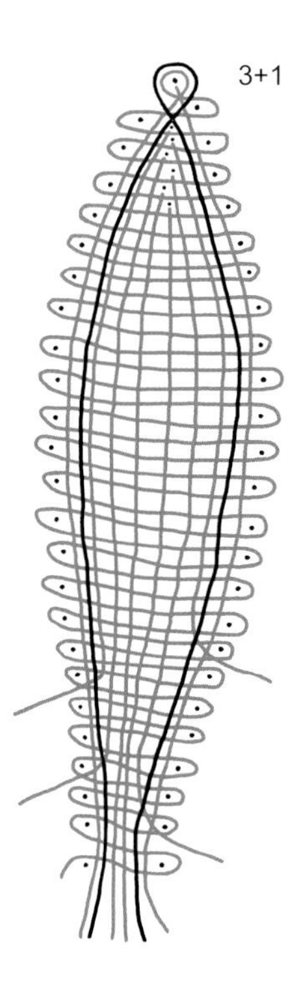

Part B

Part C
Middle petals, 2 pieces
Work as for part A. Add pairs (altogether 12) and remove as indicated.

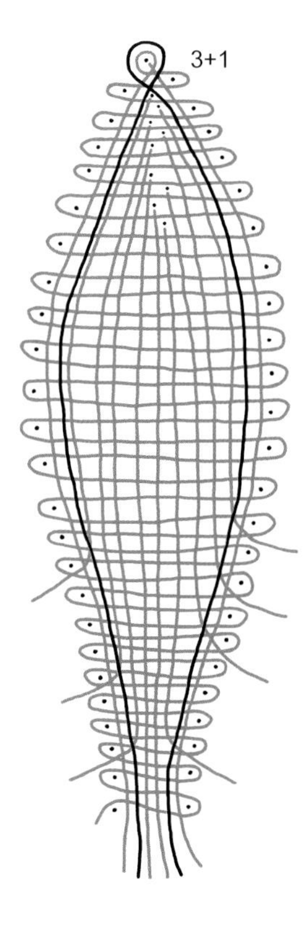

Part C

Flower no 8

Part D
Lip and fruit, 1 piece
Work the upper point in linen stitch. Start with 4 pairs light red +1 pair white workers. Remove the white workers at x on the right hand side and replace with a light red pair. Add a light red pair as workers at the split. After the split work both parts in half stitch with whole stitch edges on both sides.

Part F
Leaf, 1 piece.
Work in linen stitch. Make sewings in the middle. Start with 4 pairs hunting green + 1 bobbin matt green wire. Add pairs (altogether 6) and remove as indicated

Part G
Leaf, 1 piece.
Work in linen stitch and haf stitch. Make sewings in the middle. Start with 4 pairs hunting green + 1 bobbin matt green wire. Add pairs (altogether 6) and remove as indicated

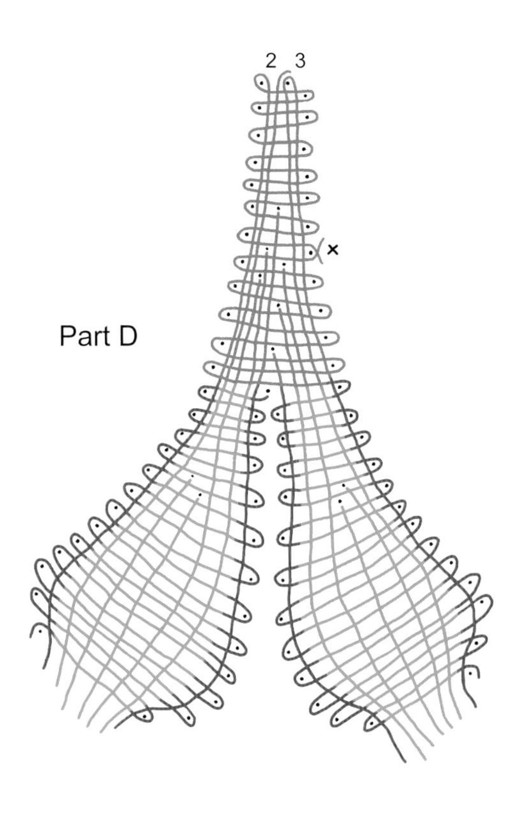

Part E
Stamens
Technique diagram for tallies see page 12.

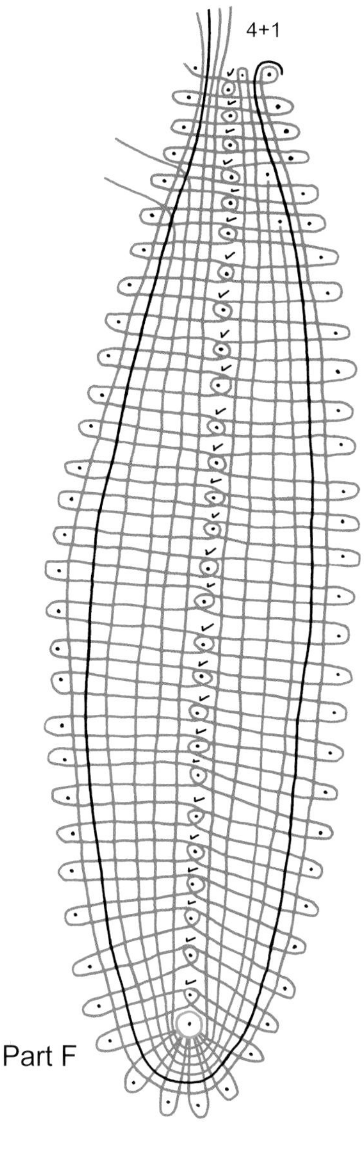

Part F

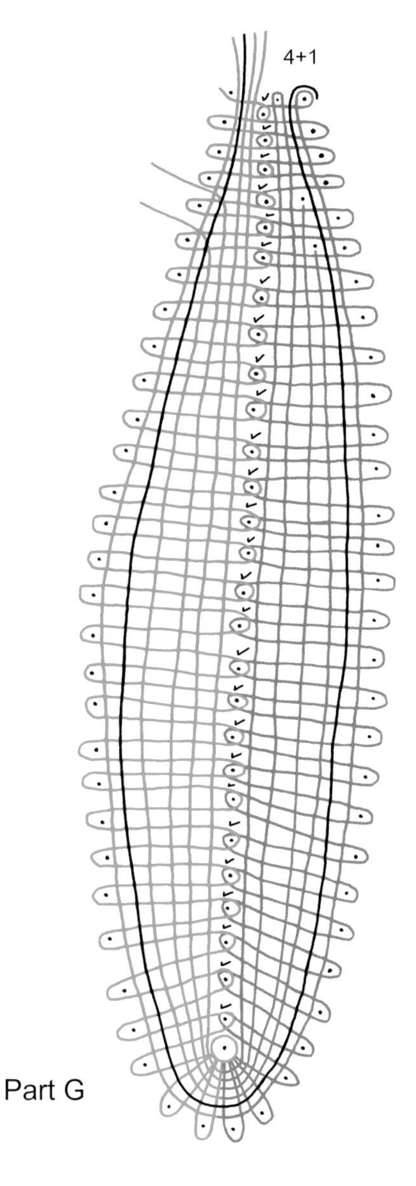

Part G

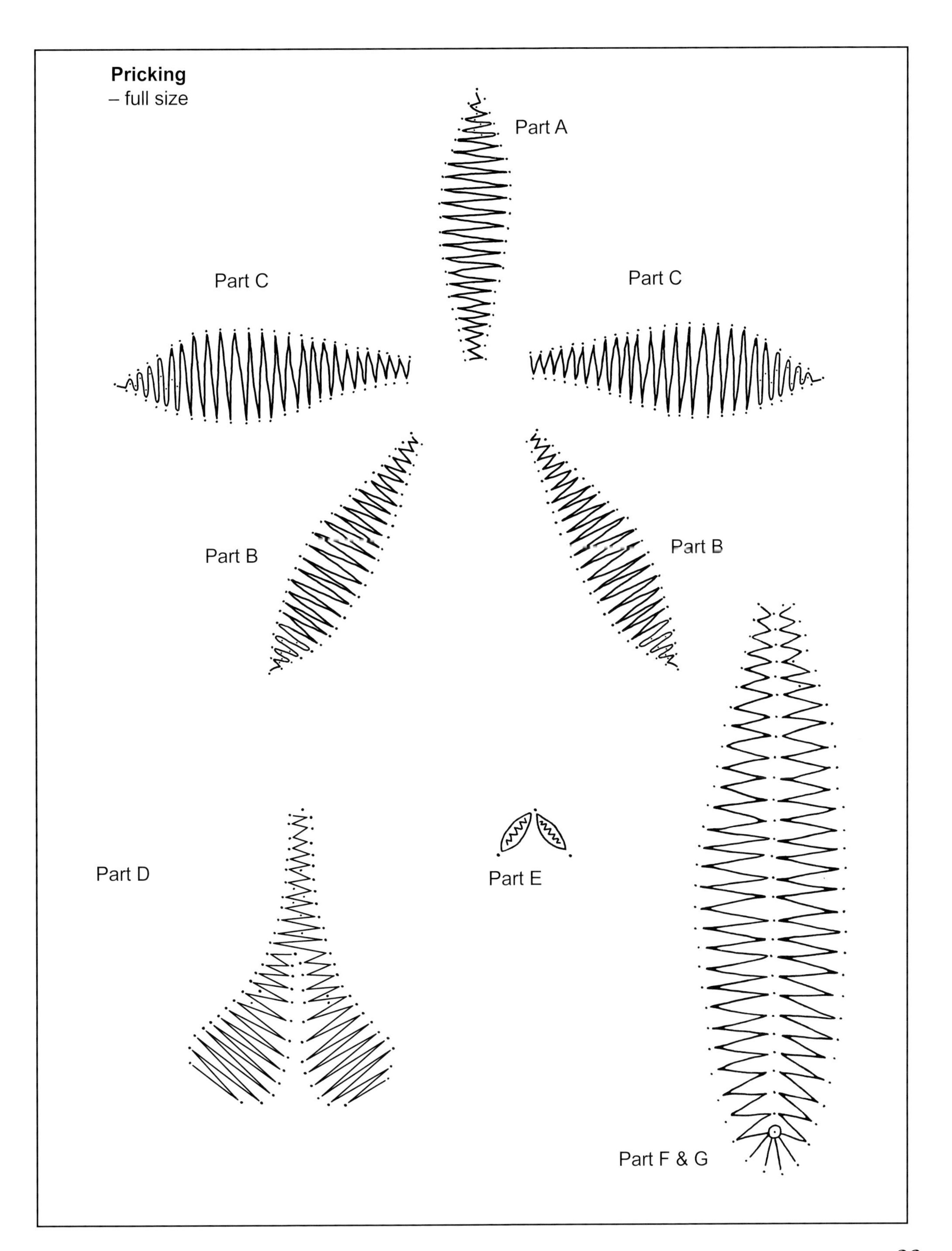
Pricking
– full size
Part A
Part C
Part C
Part B
Part B
Part D
Part E
Part F & G

Thread
Anchor col 756, light yellow
Mayflower col 1438, dark yellow
Anchor col 01, white
Goldschild col 41 hunting green

Enamelled wire
Wire 0.25mm gold
Wire 0.30mm matt green

Pairs
See text

Assembling – see page 73
Floral stub wire 0.60mm
Floral tape

Part A
Upper petal, 1 piece
Work in linen stitch. Start with 3 pairs light yellow. Add pairs (altogether 10) and remove as indicated.

Part B
Middle petals, 2 pieces
Work in half stitch with whole stitch edges on both sides. Make sewings in the middle. Start with 4 pairs light yellow + 1 bobbin gold wire. Add pairs (altogether 7) and remove as indicated.

Part C
Lower petals, 2 pieces
Work in linen stitch. Start with 3 pairs light yellow. Add pairs (altogether 10) and remove as indicated.

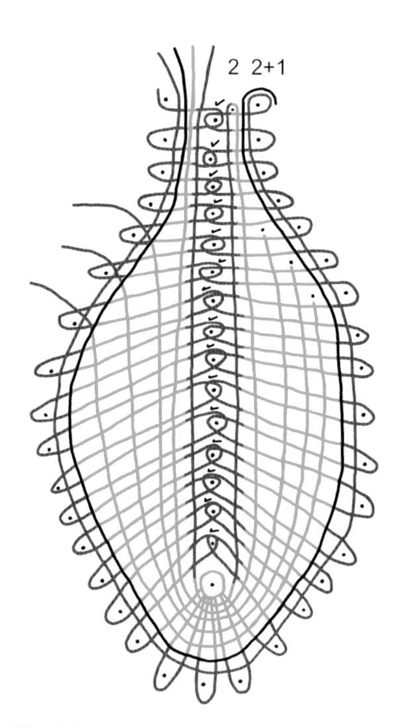

Part B

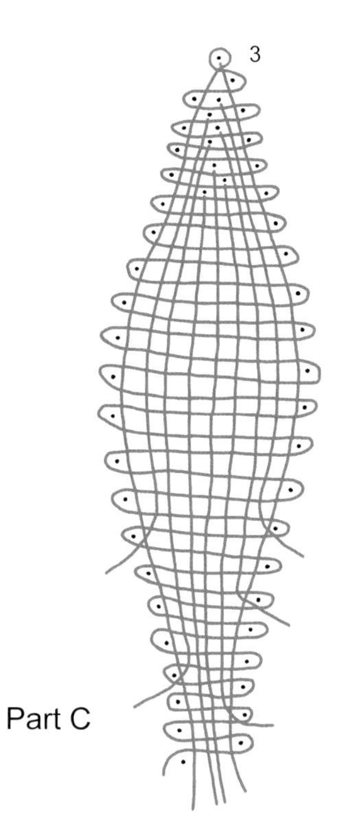

Part C

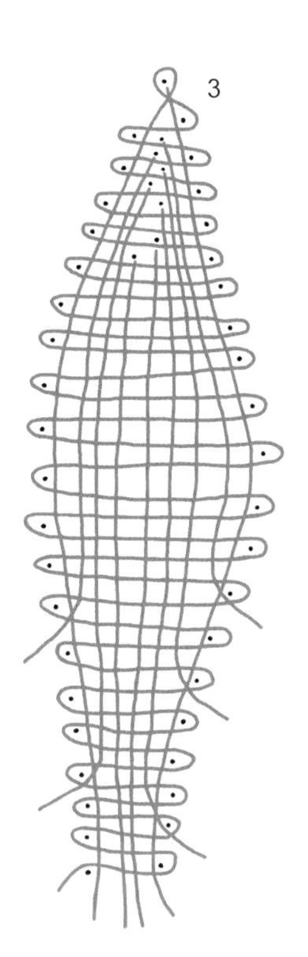

Part A

Flower no 9

Part D

Lip, stamens and fruit, 1 piece

Work the cross piece in linen stitch with whole stitch edges. Start with 8 pairs dark yellow. For the vertical parts, add pairs to the cross piece in the following order:

2 pairs dark yellow
1 pair dark yellow
2 pairs dark yellow
2 pairs white
1 pair dark yellow
2 pairs dark yellow
1 pair dark yellow
2 pairs dark yellow (one of these pairs is the workers)

Work in linen stitch. Begin working across all 3 parts. Add 1 pair yellow workers to the left hand part and 1 pair white workers to the middle part and then work the parts separately.

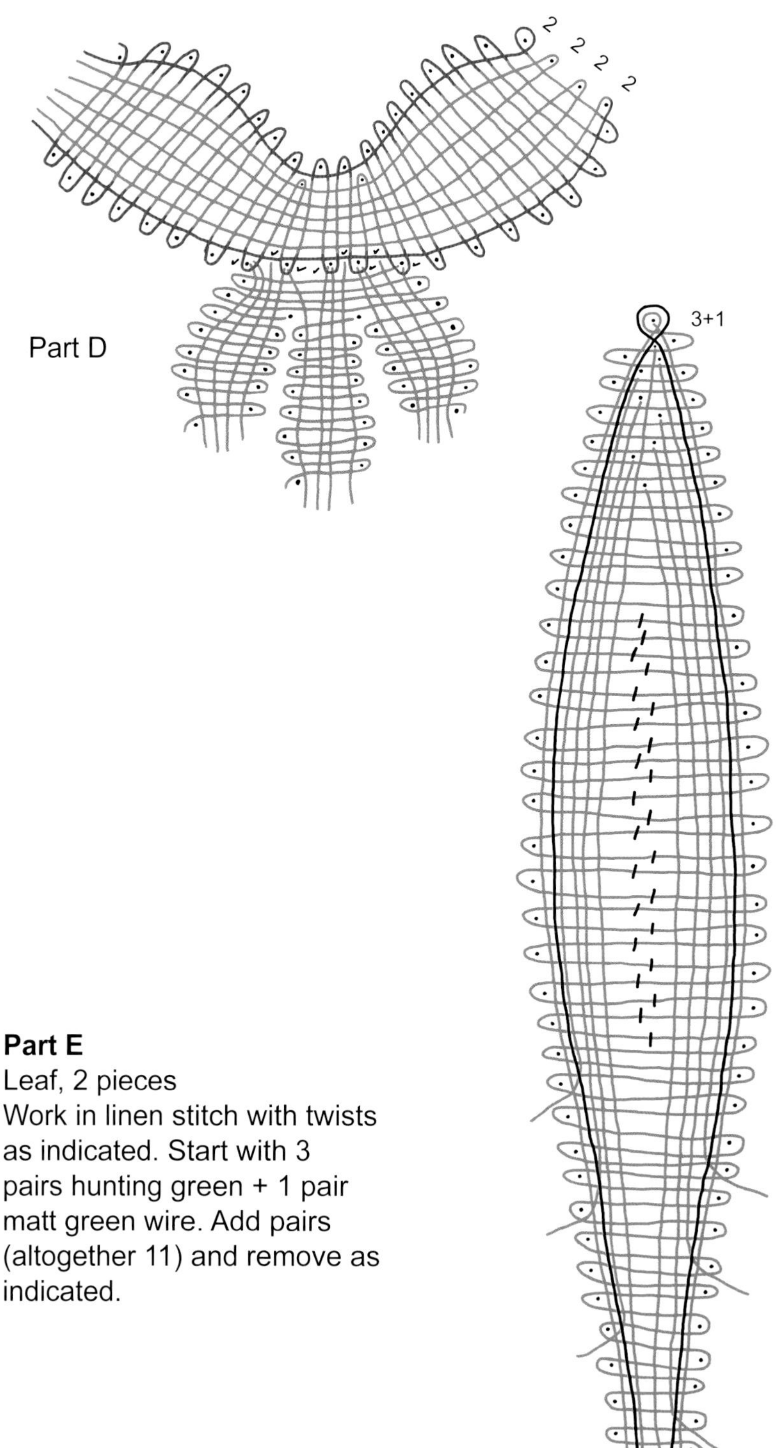

Part E

Leaf, 2 pieces

Work in linen stitch with twists as indicated. Start with 3 pairs hunting green + 1 pair matt green wire. Add pairs (altogether 11) and remove as indicated.

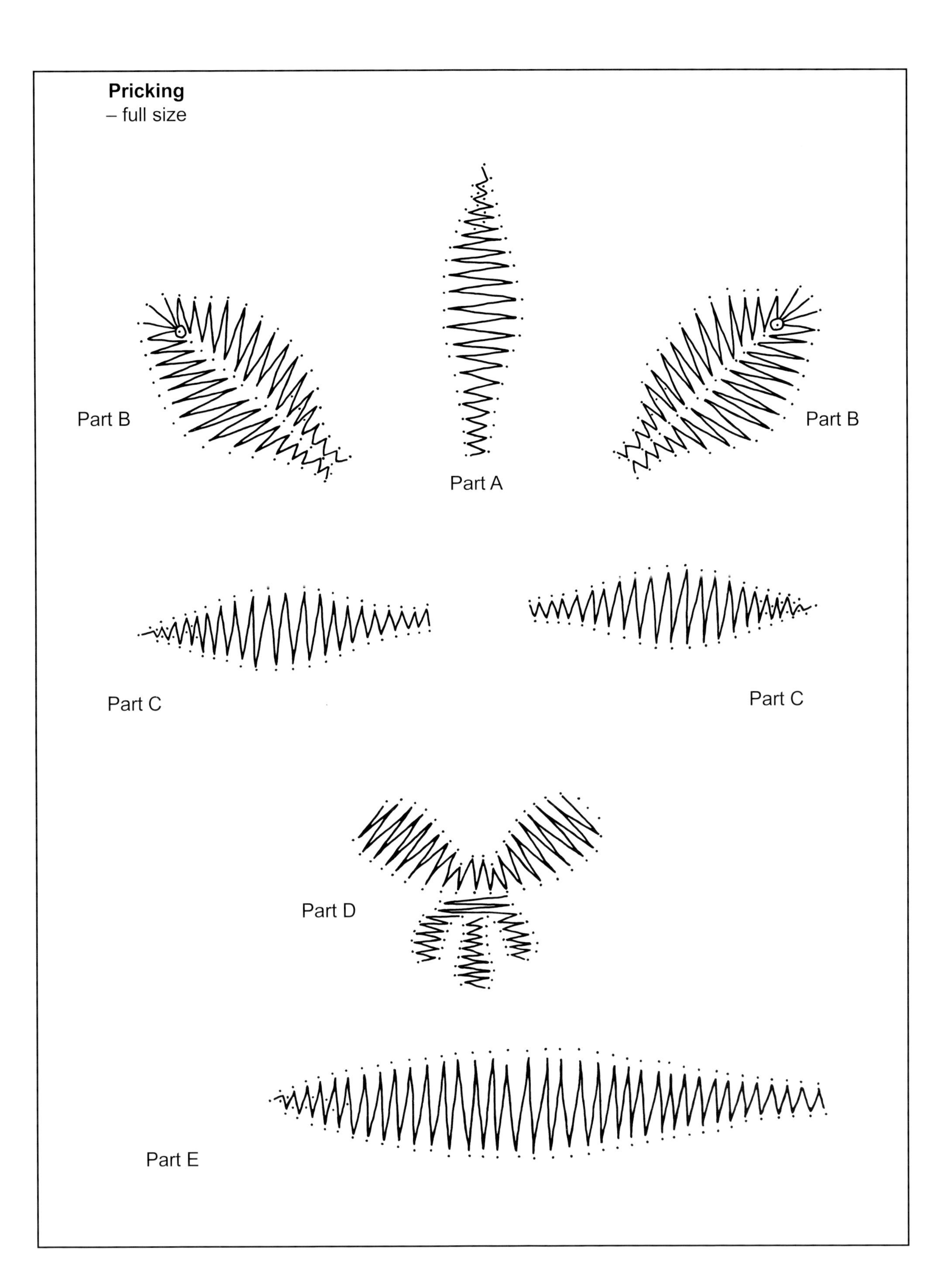
Pricking
– full size
Part B
Part A
Part B
Part C
Part C
Part D
Part E

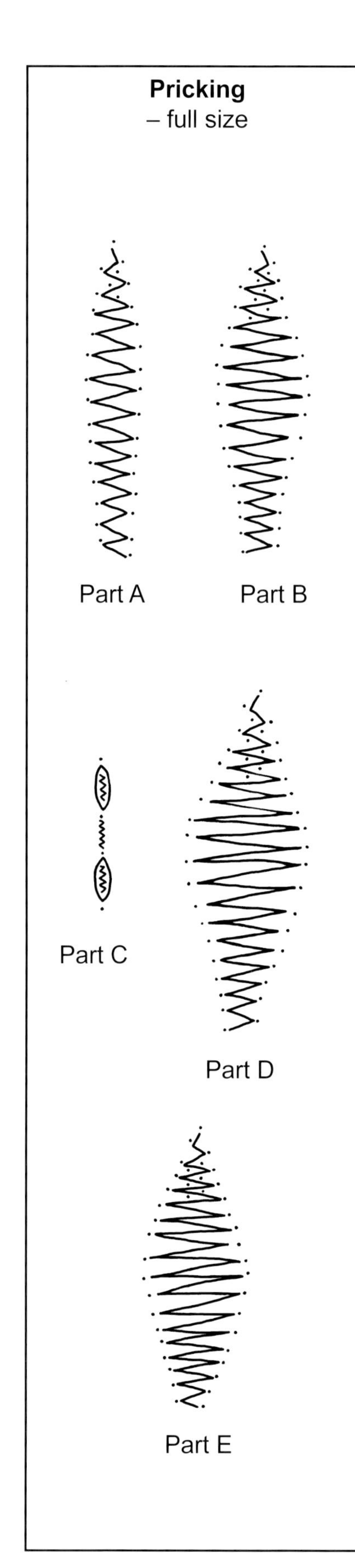

Thread
Anchor col 108, lilac
Anchor col 259, light green
Mayflower col 5520, green

Enamelled wire
Wire 0.25mm light lilac
Wire 0.25mm May green

Pairs
See text

Assembling – see page 74
Floral stub wire 0.60mm
Floral tape

Part A
Inner petals, 4 pieces
Work in linen stitch. Start with 3 pairs light lilac +1 pair light lilac wire. Add pairs as shown (altogether 6 pairs).

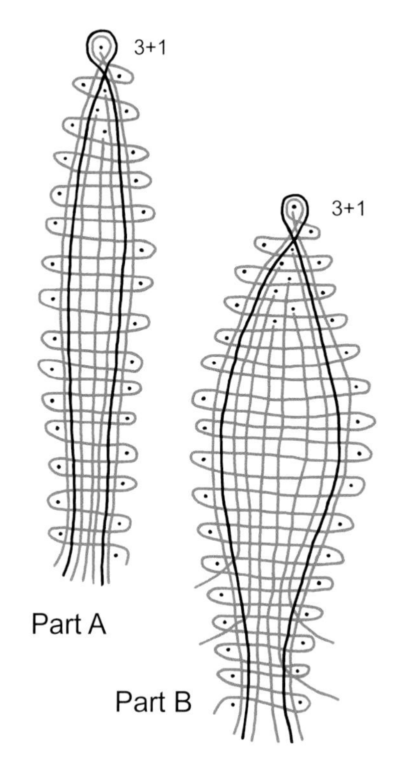

Part B
Outer petals, 4 pieces
Work as for part A. Add pairs (altogether 9) and remove as indicated.

Part C
Stamens, 7 pieces
Work tallies with plaits in between, using 2 pairs light green. See technique diagram for tallies page 12.

Part D
Large leaf, 1piece
Work in linen stitch with twists as indicated. Start with 4 pairs green + 1 pair May green wire. Add pairs (altogether 11 pairs) and remove as indicated.

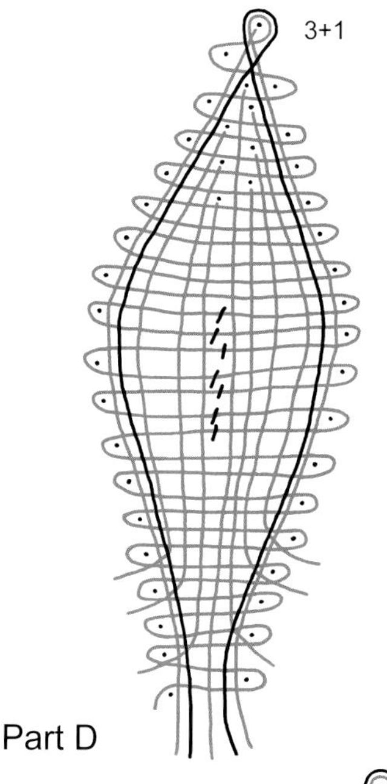

Part E
Small leaf, 2 pieces
Work as for part D. Start with 3 pairs green + 1 pair May green wire. Add pairs (altogether 9 pairs) and remove as indicated.

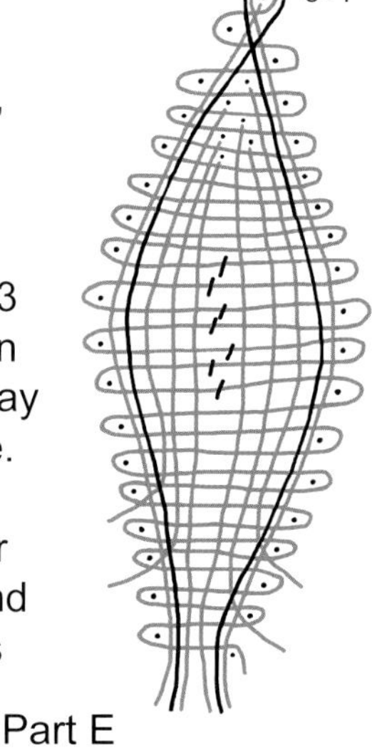

Flower no 10

Pricking
– full size

Part A

Part B

Part C

Part D

Thread
Mayflower col 1120, orange
Goldschild col 41 hunting green

Enamelled wire
Wire 0.25mm copper
Wire 0.30mm matt green

Pairs
See text

Assembling – see page 74
Floral stub wire 0.60mm
Floral tape

Part A
Petals, 3 pieces per flower
Work in linen stitch. Start with 3 pairs orange + 1 pair copper wire. Add pairs (altogether 9 pairs) and remove as indicated.

Part B, C, D
Leaves, 1 of each per stem.
Work in linen stitch with twists as indicated. Start with 3 pairs hunting green + 1 pair matt green wire.
Add and remove pairs as indicated.
In part B
– 11 pairs
In part C
– 13 pairs
In part D
– 13 pairs.

3+1

Part B

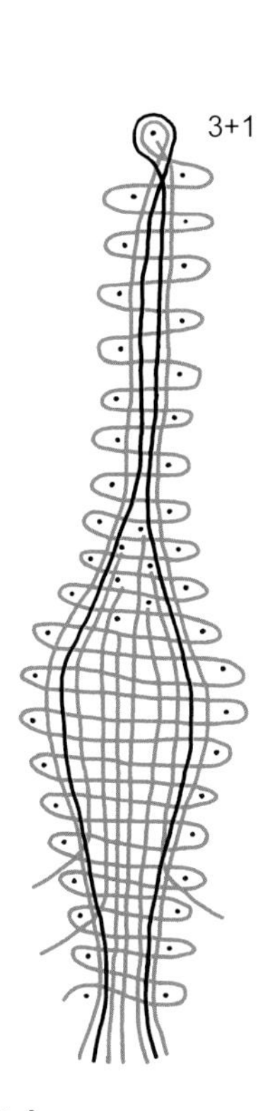

Part A

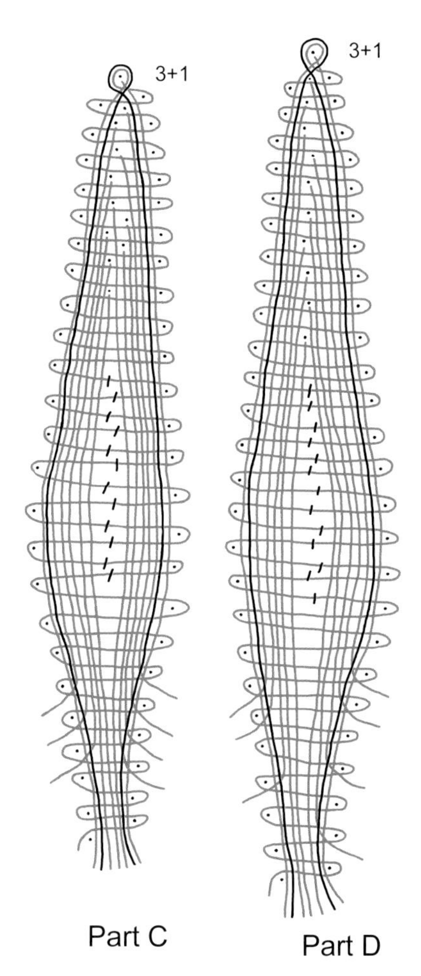

Part C

Part D

Flower no 11

Pricking
– full size

Part A

Part B

Part C

Thread
Goldschild col 51, dark blue

Enamelled wire
Wire 0.25mm, blue

Assembling – see page 75
Floral stub wire 0.60mm
Floral tape

&
Güttermann glass beads 6mm, matt blue

Part A
Split petal, 3 pieces
Work in linen stitch. Start at the left split with 3 pairs thread + 1 pair wire. Add pairs as indicated (altogether 9). Then start the right split with 3 pairs thread + 1 pair wire. Add pairs as indicated (altogether 6). Twist the enamelled pairs meeting at the middle before cutting them off. Continue the lace and cut the wire with an 8cm tail.

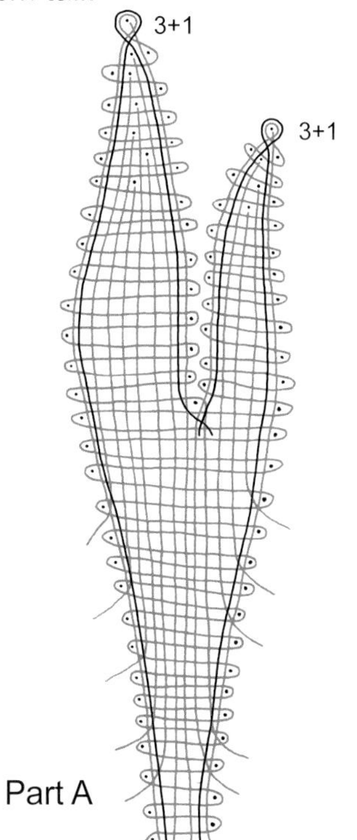

Part B
Inner petals, 3 pieces
Work in linen stitch. Start with 3 pairs thread + 1 pair wire. Add pairs (altogether 9 pairs) and remove as indicated.

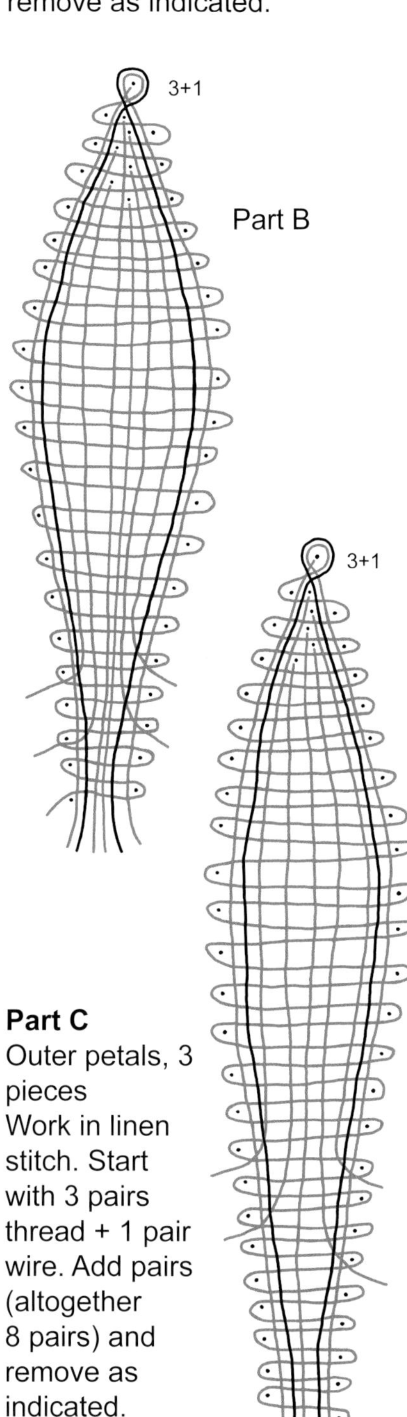

Part C
Outer petals, 3 pieces
Work in linen stitch. Start with 3 pairs thread + 1 pair wire. Add pairs (altogether 8 pairs) and remove as indicated.

Flower no 12

Thread
Venus col 195, red/brown
Goldschild col 41, hunting green

Enamelled wire
Wire 0.25mm, red/brown
Wire 0.30mm, matt green

&
Mini beads, red/brown

Pairs
See text

Assembling – see page75
Floral stub wire 0.60mm
Floral tape

&
Stamens no S.16
Hobby paint, yellow

Part A
Inner petals, 3 pieces
Work in linen stitch. Start with 3 pairs red/brown thread + 1 pair red/brown wire. Thread 4-5 beads on the workers and place randomly in the lace. Add pairs (altogether 7 pairs) and remove as indicated.

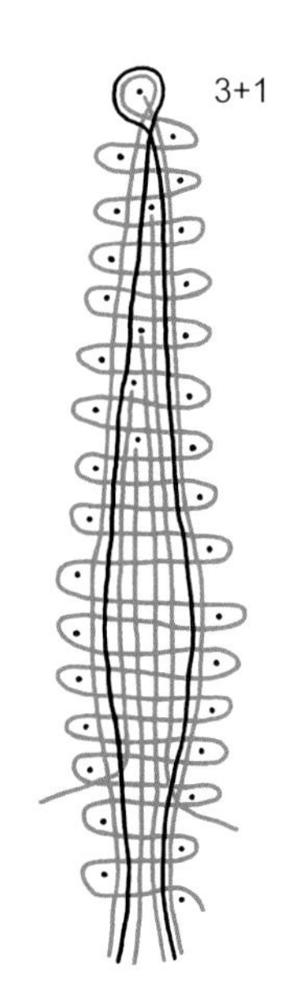

Part B
Middle petals, 3 pieces
Work as for part A. Start with 4 pairs red/brown thread + 1 pair red/brown wire. Thread 6-7 beads on the workers. Add pairs (altogether 13 pairs) and remove as indicated.

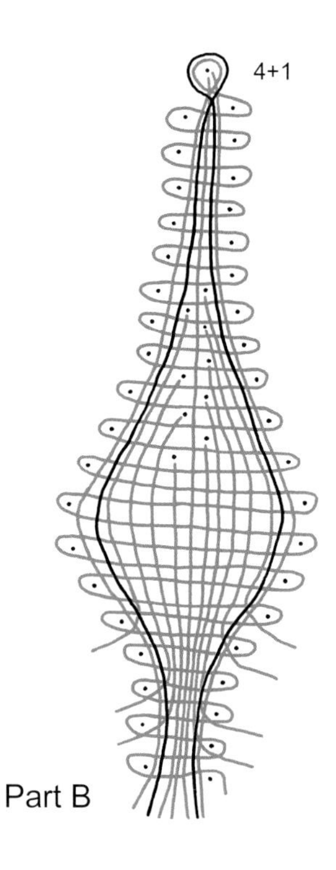

Part C
Outer petals, 3 pieces
Work as for part A. Start with 4 pairs red/brown thread + 1 pair red/brown wire. Thread 8-9 beads on the workers. Add pairs (altogether 15 pairs) and remove as indicated.

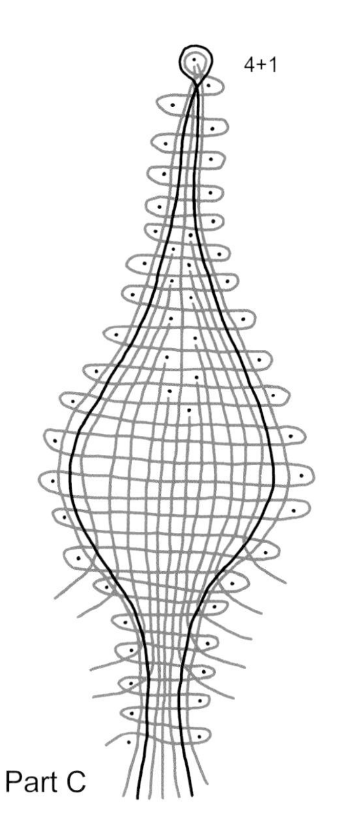

Flower no 13

Part D
Bud petals, 3 pieces
Work in linen stitch. Start with 3 pairs re/brown thread + 1 pair red/brown wire. Add pairs as indicated (altogether 5).

Part E
Leaf, 1 piece
Work in linen stitch. Start with 4 pairs hunting green + 1 pair matt green wire. Add pairs (altogether 11 pairs) and remove as indicated.'

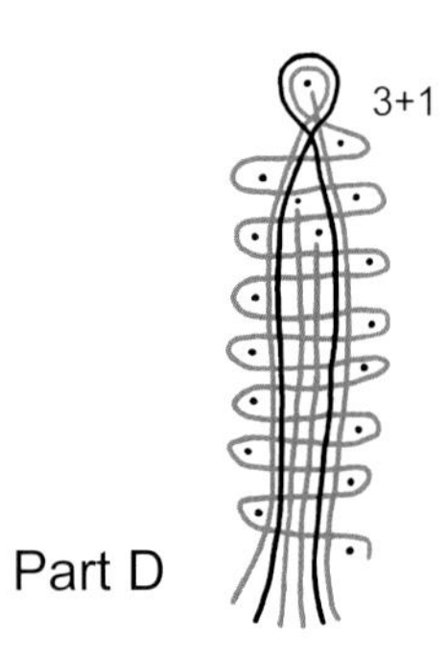

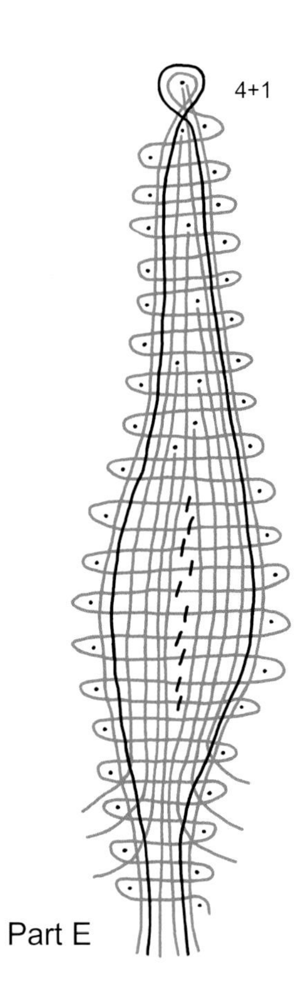

Pricking
– full size

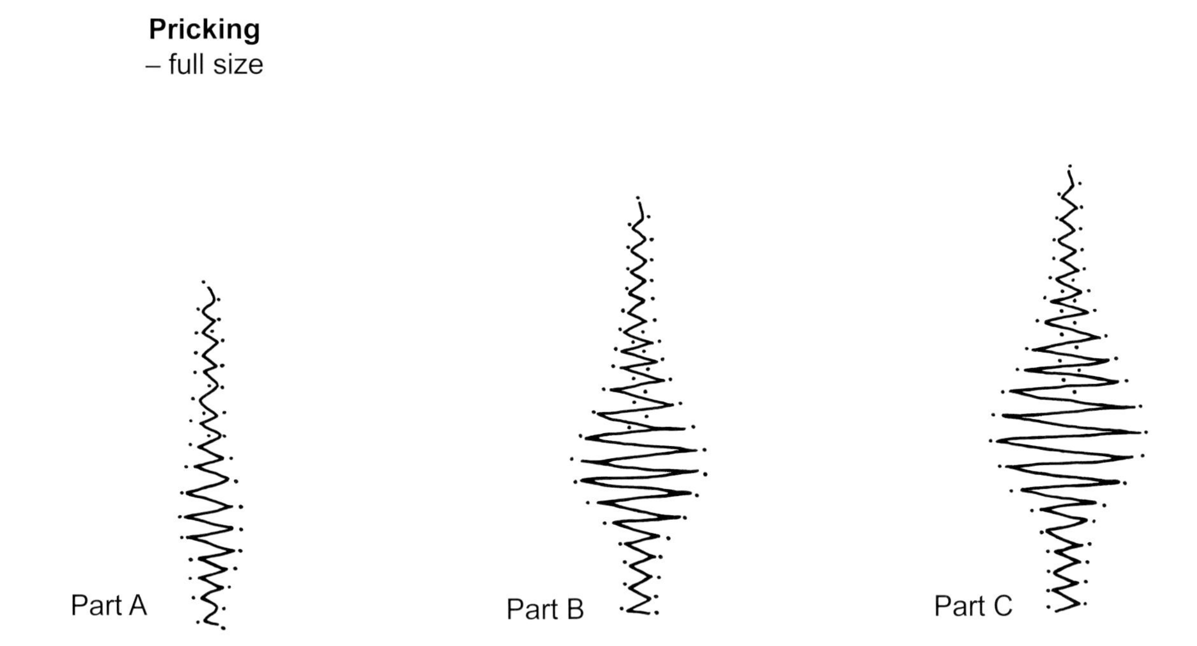

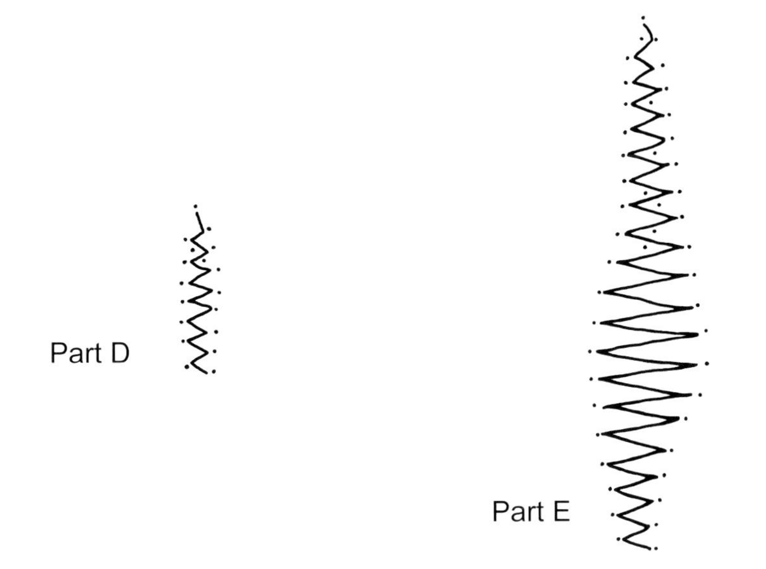

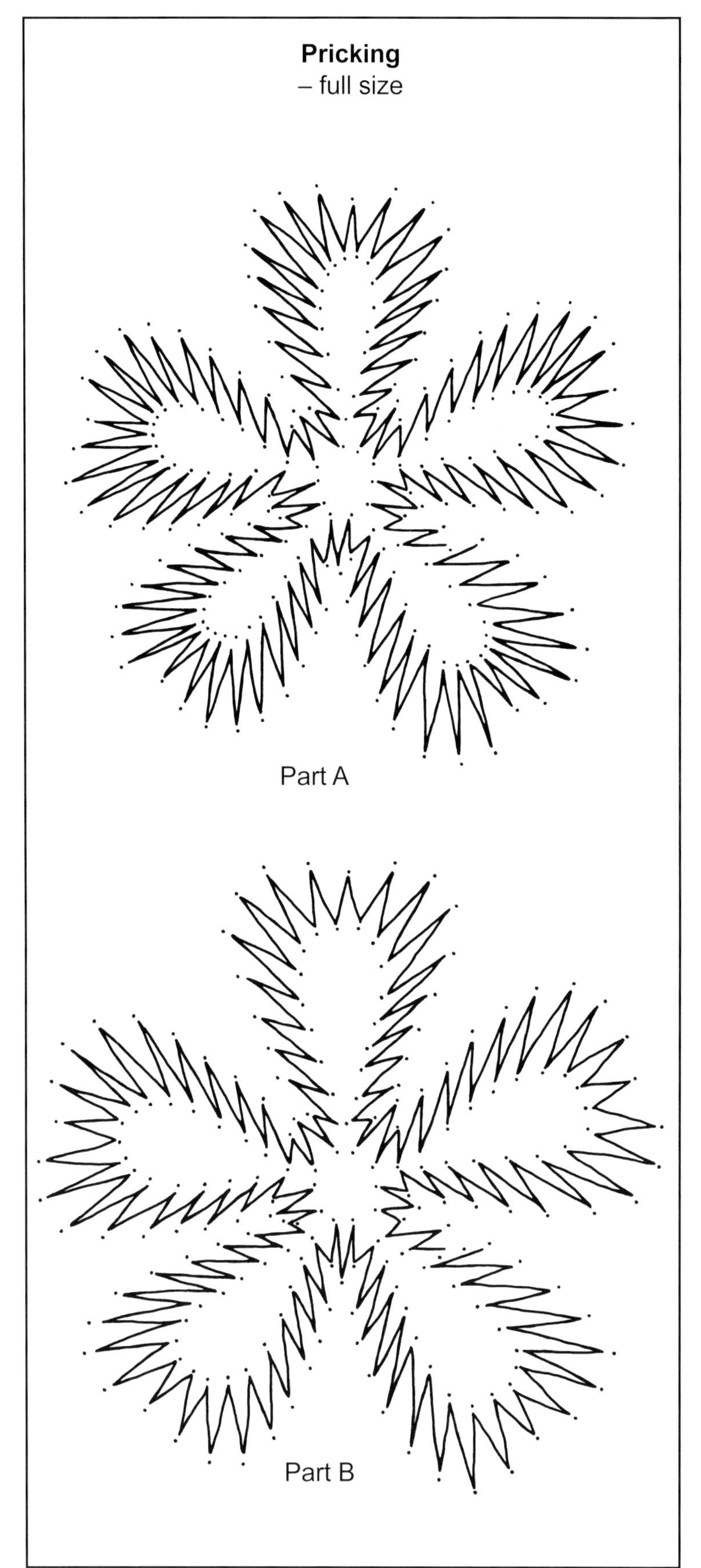

Thread
Goldschild col 51, dark blue

Enamelled wire
Wire 0.25mm, blue

Pairs
See text

&
Gütermann glass beads, matt blue 6mm

Assembling- see page 76
Floral stub wire 0.60mm
Floral tape

Part A
Inner petals, 2 pieces
Work in half stitch with whole stitch on both edges. Use 5 pairs thread +1 bobbin wire. Join the finish to the start and tie off with reef knots.

Part B
Outer petal, 2 pieces
Work as for part A, with 6 pairs thread and 1 bobbin wire.

Part A

Flower no 14

Pricking
– full size

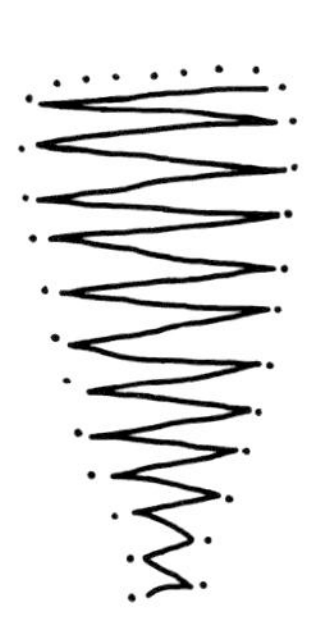

Part A

Part B

Part C

Thread
DMC col 210, light lilac
Venus col 675, dark lilac
Mayflower col 1438, dark yellow

Enamelled wire
Wire 0.25mm, light lilac
Wire 0.25mm dark lilac

Pairs
See text

Assembling – see page 76
Floral stub wire 0.60mm
Floral tape

Part A
Lip, 1 piece
Work in linen stitch with twists as indicated. Start with 11 pairs dark lilac + 1 pair dark lilac wire. Remove pairs as indicated.

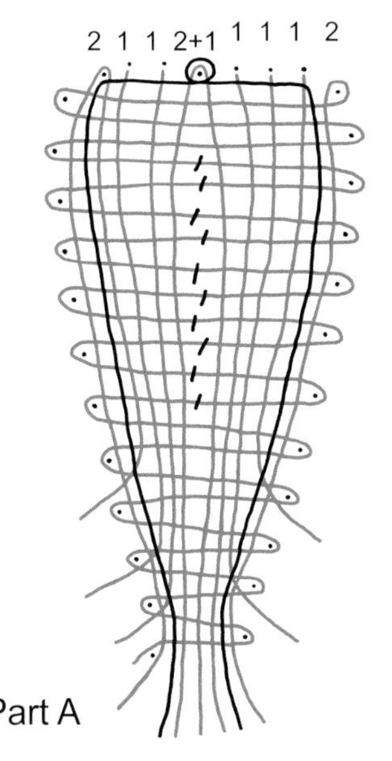

Part A

Part B
Fruit bud, 1 piece
Work in linen stitch. Use 7 pairs dark yellow. Remove pairs as indicated.

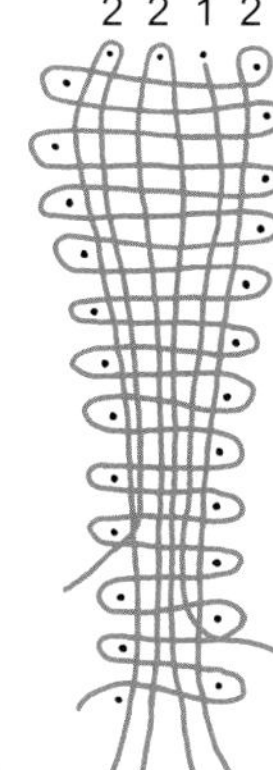

Part B

Part C
Petals, 5 pieces
Work in linen stitch. Start with 4 pairs light lilac + 1 pair light lilac wire. Add pairs (altogether 6 pairs) and remove as indicated.

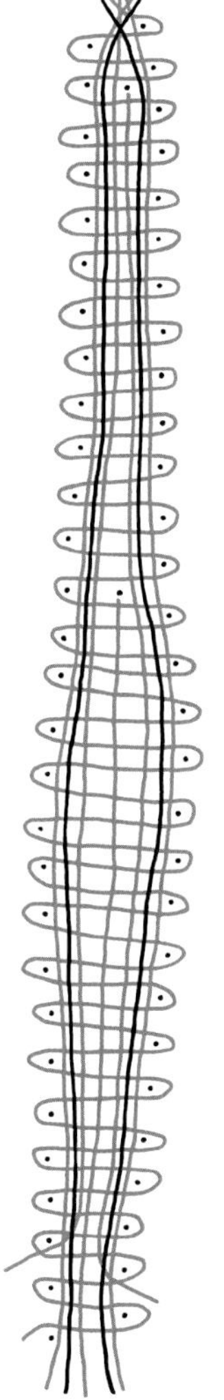

Part C

Flower no 15

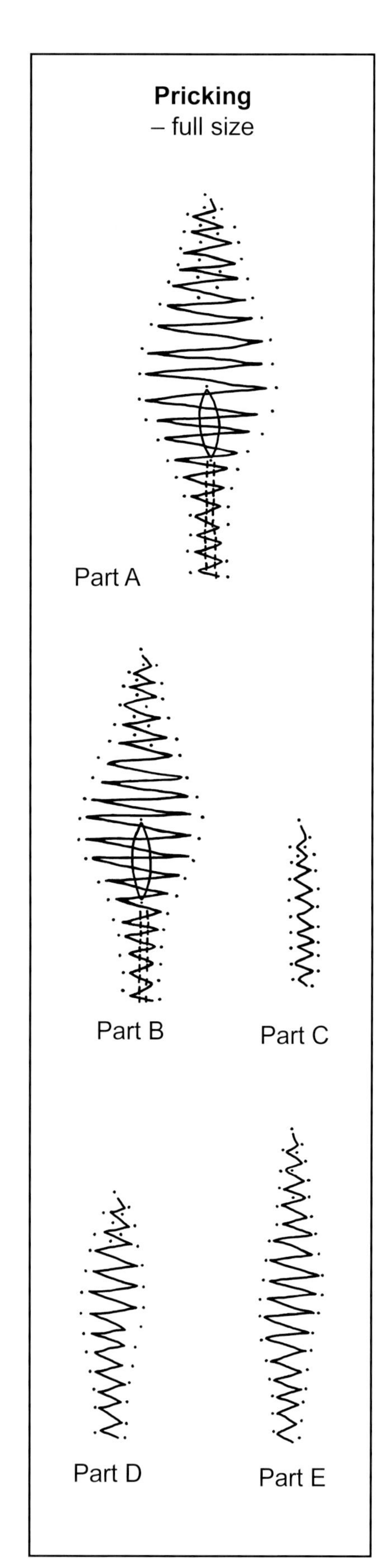

Thread
Anchor col 249, yellow
Venus col EM 500, dark lilac
Goldschild col 41, hunting green

Enamelled wire
Wire 0.25mm, dark lilac
Wire 0.30mm, matt green

Pairs
See text

Assembling – see page 77
Floral stub wire 0.60mm
Floral tape

Part A
Outer petals, 3 pieces
Work in linen stitch. Start with 3 pairs dark lilac + 1 pair lilac wire. Add pairs as indicated (altogether 13 pairs). Add 2 pairs yellow as indicated, where the almond shape narrows. Work a tally as illustrated on page 12. Continue with the lilac pairs and incorporate the 2 yellow pairs in the middle. Remove pairs as indicated.

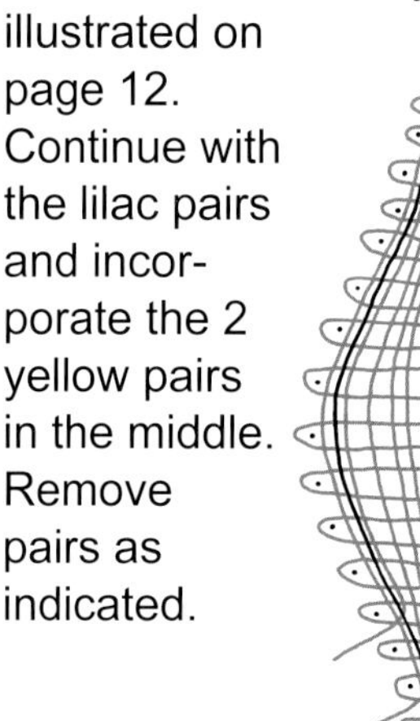

Part B
Inner petals, 3 pieces
Work as Part A. Start with 3 pairs dark lilac + 1 pair lilac wire. Add pairs (altogether 11 pairs) and remove as indicated.

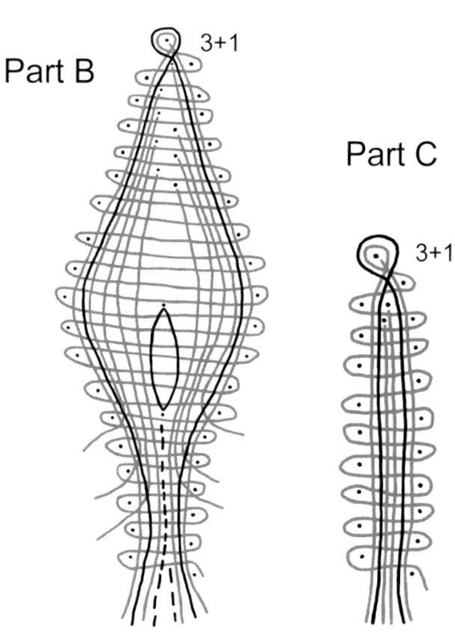

Part C
Small petals, 3 pieces
Work in linen stitch. Start with 3 pairs dark lilac + 1 pair lilac wire. Add pairs (altogether 5 pairs) as indicated.

Part D
Bud petals, 3 pieces
Work in linen stitch. Start with 4 pairs dark lilac + 1 pair lilac wire. Add pairs (altogether 8 pairs) and remove as indicated.

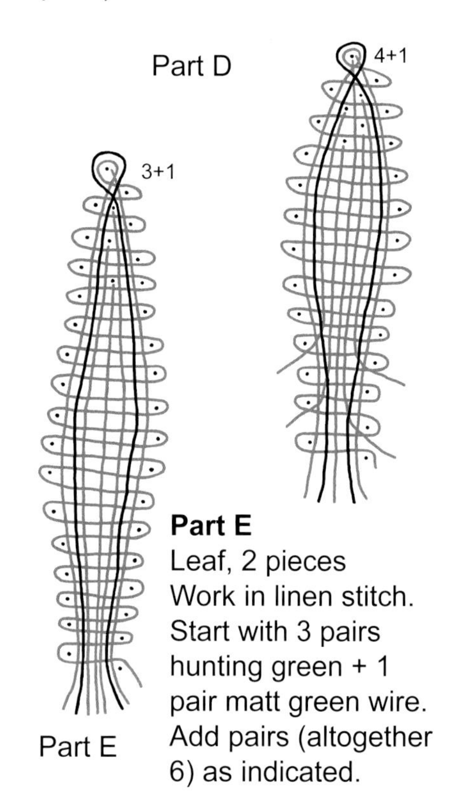

Part E
Leaf, 2 pieces
Work in linen stitch. Start with 3 pairs hunting green + 1 pair matt green wire. Add pairs (altogether 6) as indicated.

Flower no 16

Thread
DMC col 3608, pink
Goldschild col 41, hunting green

Enamelled wire
Wire 0.25mm, light red
Wire 0.30mm matt green

Pairs
See text

Assembling – see page 77
Floral stub wire 0.60mm
Floral tape

&
Stamens no S.06

Part A
Outer petals 1 piece
Work in linen stitch with whole stitch edges. Use 6 pairs pink + 1 bobbin light red wire.

Part B
Middle petals, 1 piece
Work as for part A. Use 6 pairs pink + 1 bobbin light red wire

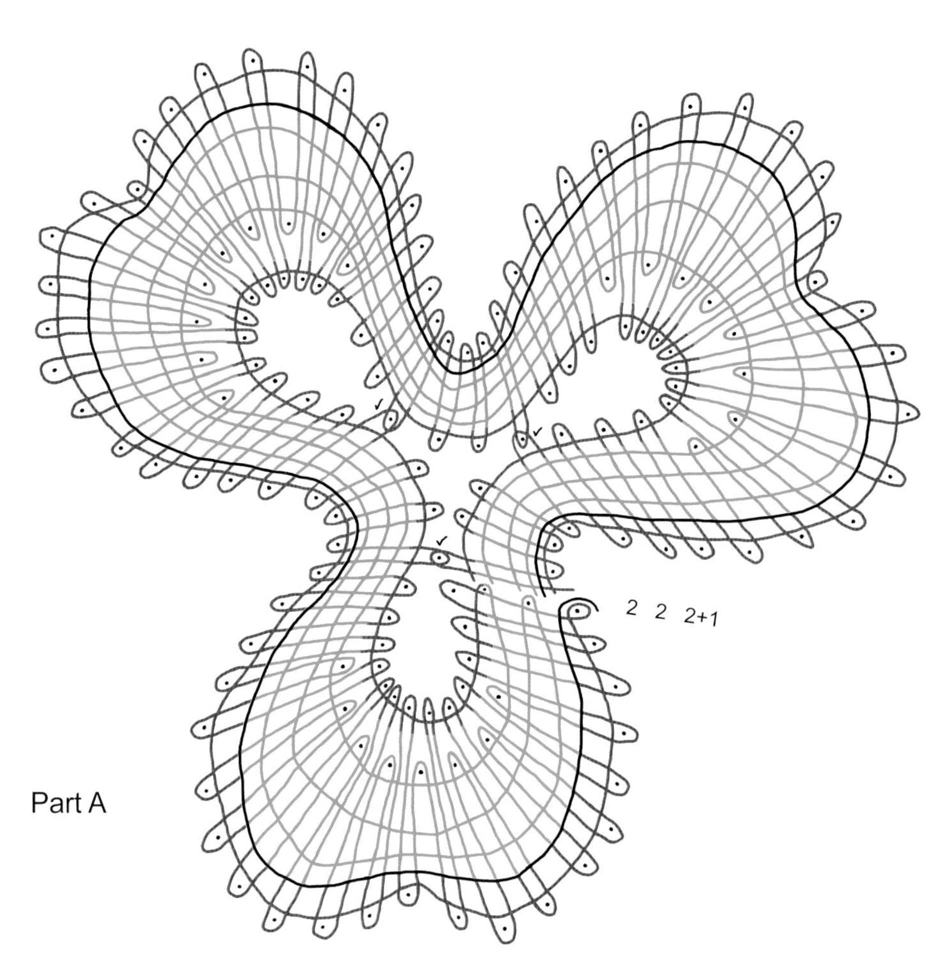

Part A

Flower no 17

Part C
Inner petals, 3 pieces
Work in linen stitch. Start with 3 pairs pink + 1 pair light red wire. Add pairs (altogether 6) as indicated.

Part D
Leaf, 3-5 pieces
Work in linen stitch with twists as indicated. Start with 3 pairs hunting green + 1 pair matt green wire. Add pairs (altogether 9 pairs) and remove as indicated.

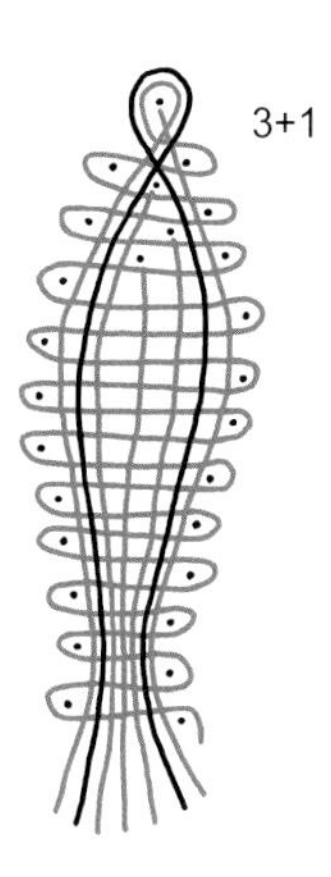

Part C

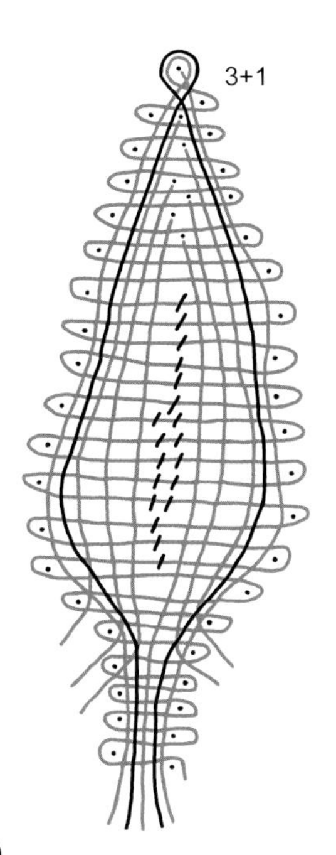

Part D

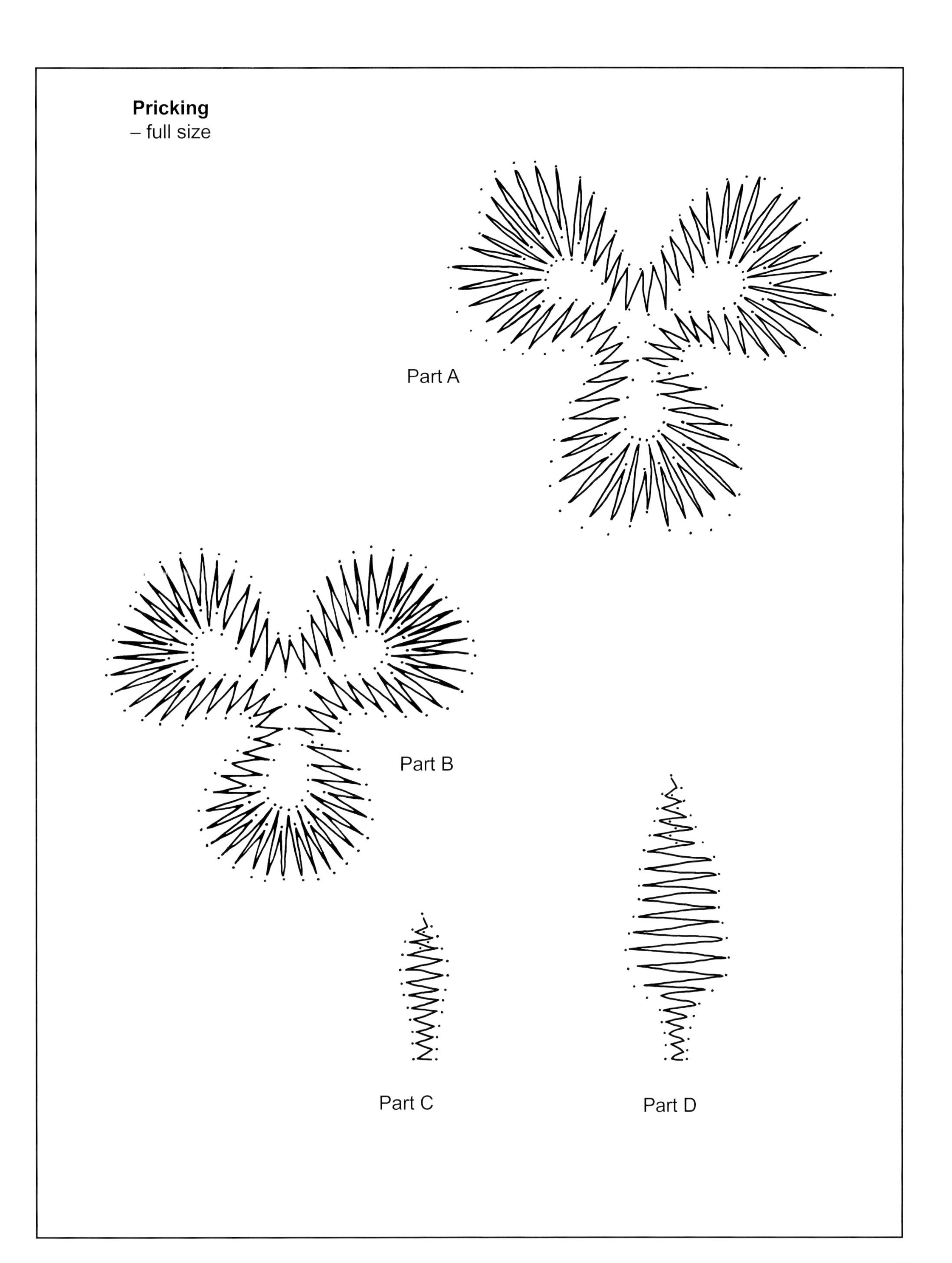
Pricking
– full size
Part A
Part B
Part C
Part D

Thread
Mayflower col 5520, green
Venus col EM 500, lilac
Goldschild col 41, hunting green

Enamelled wire
Wire 0.25mm, May green and lilac
Wire 0.30mm, matt green

Pairs
See text

Assembling – see page 78
Floral stub wire 0.60mm
Floral tape

Part A
Upper petal, 1 piece
Work in linen stitch. Start with 3 pairs green + 1 pair May green wire. Add pairs as indicated (altogether 9 pairs) and remove as indicated.

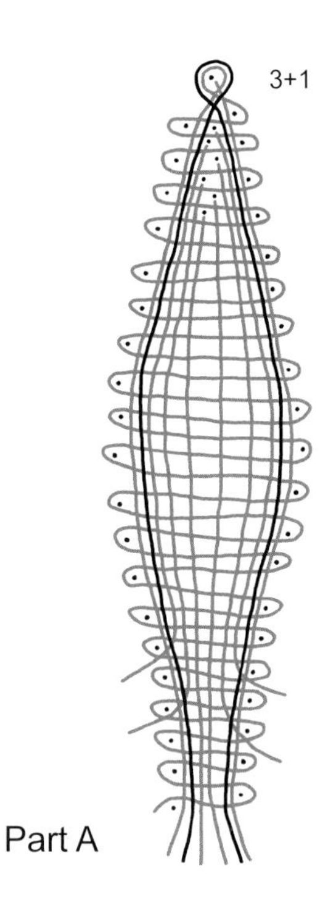

Part B
Middle petals, 2 pieces
Work in linen stitch. Start with 4 pairs green + 1 pair May green wire. Add pairs (altogether 14 pairs) and remove as indicated.

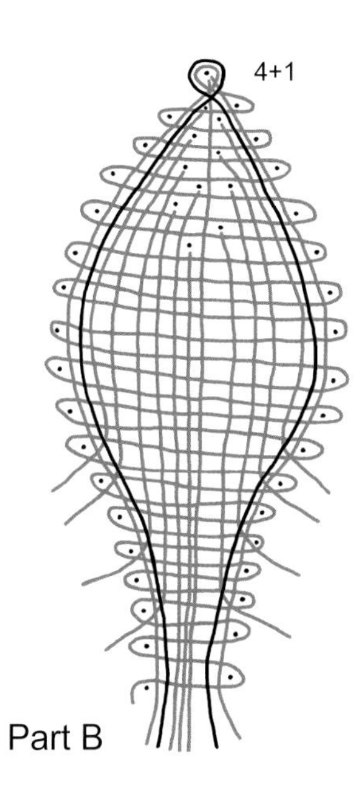

Part C
Lower petals, 2 pieces
Work in linen stitch. Start with 3 pairs green + 1 pair May green wire. Add pairs (altogether 10 pairs) and remove as indicated.

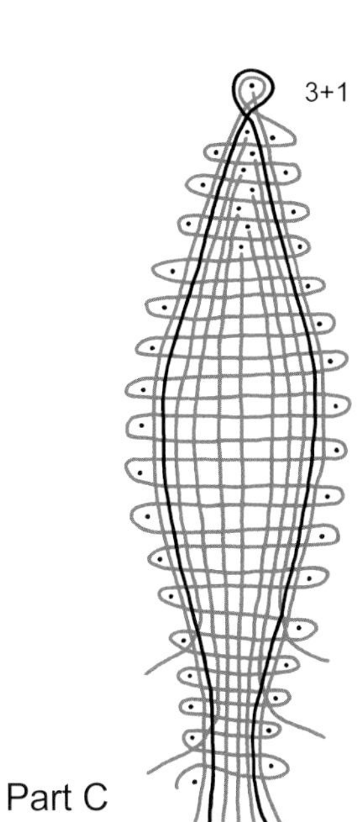

Part D
Fruit bud 1 piece
Work in linen stitch with 6 pairs green

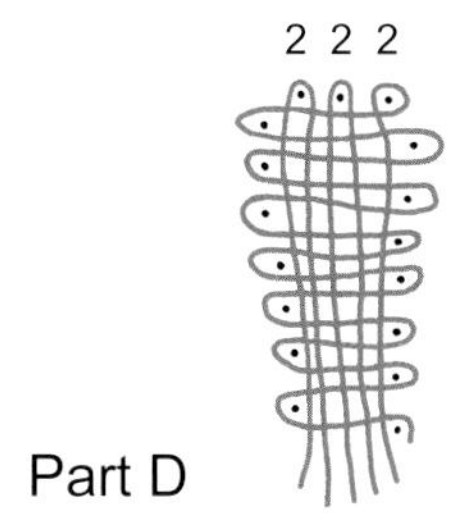

Part E
Lip, 1 piece
Work in linen stitch. Start at the point of the inner part with 4 pairs lilac + 1 pair lilac wire. Work the outer border in half stitch with a whole stitch edge, using 4 pairs lilac. Make sewings to the inner part.

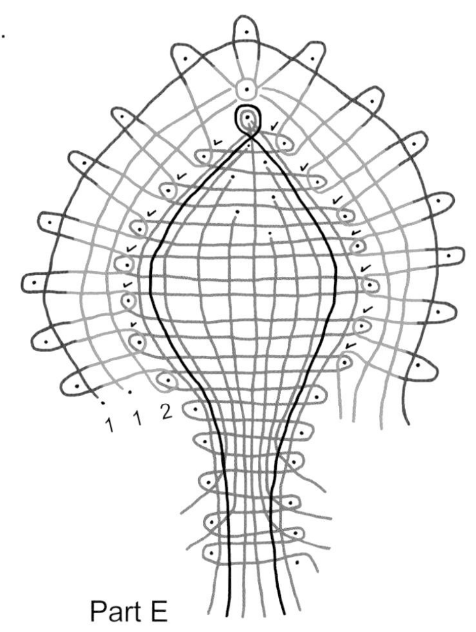

Flower no 18

Part F
Stamens, 2 pieces
Work in linen stitch. Start with 4 pairs lilac + 1 pair lilac wire. Add pairs (altogether 6 pairs) as indicated.

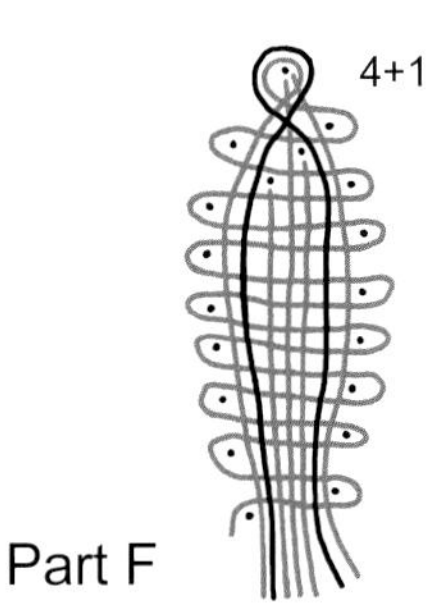

Part G
Bud petals, 3 pieces
Work in linen stitch. Start with 4 pairs green + 1 pair May green wire. Add pairs (altogether 8 pairs) and remove as indicated.

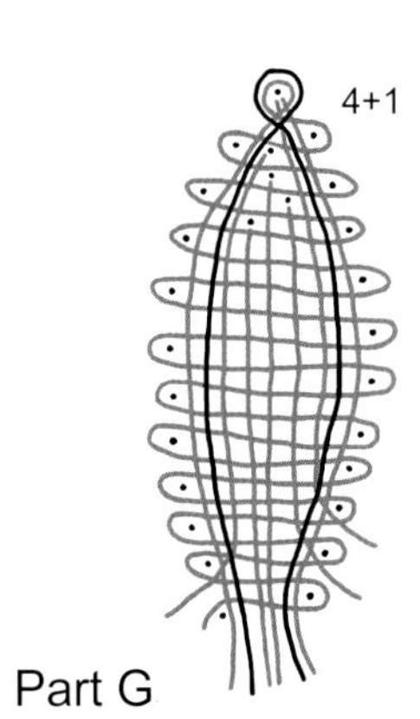

Part H
Big leaves, 2 pieces
Work in linen stitch. Start with 4 pairs hunting green +1 pair matt green wire. Add pairs (altogether 13 pairs) and remove as indicated.

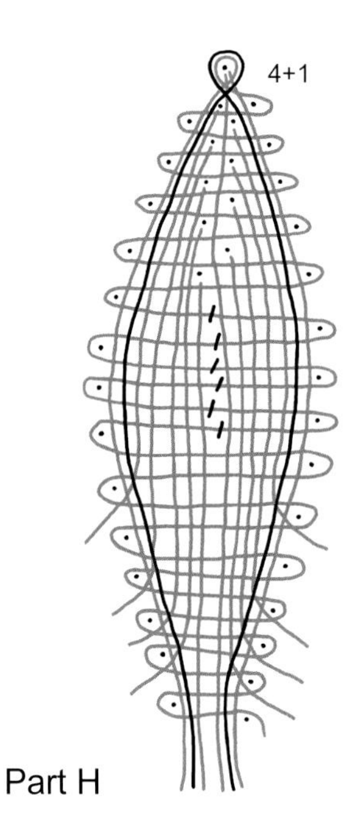

Part I
Small leaves, 2 pieces
Work in linen stitch with twists as indicated. Start with 3 pairs hunting green + 1 pair matt green wire. Add pairs (altogether 9 pairs) and remove as indicated

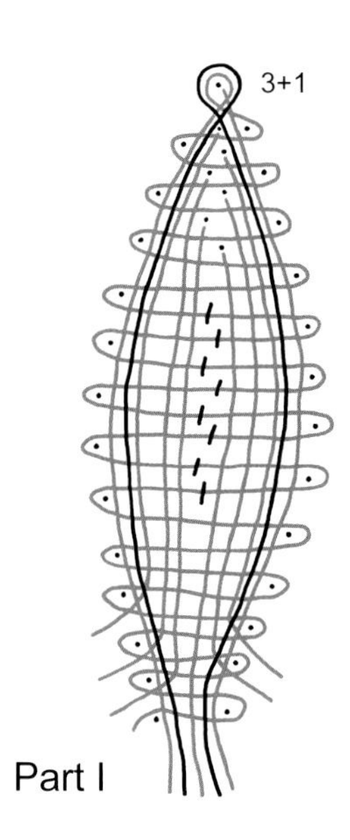

Pricking
– full size
Part A
Part B
Part B
Part C
Part C
Part D
Part E
Part F
Part G
Part H
Part I

Flower 1 – assembling

1. Lap the petals over each other to form a fan. Stitch them together at the base. Form a hole at the base with a darning needle. Bend a floral stub wire in half and put it through the pre-formed hole.

2. Press and twist the wire firmly together. The wire is stiff and it is an advantage to use a small pair of pointed pliers to grip the wire.

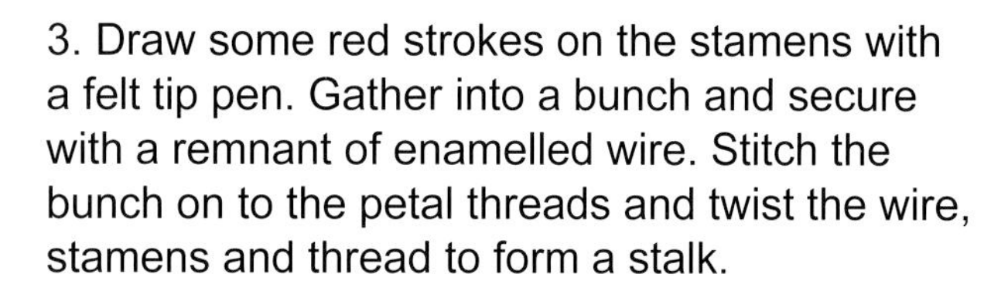

3. Draw some red strokes on the stamens with a felt tip pen. Gather into a bunch and secure with a remnant of enamelled wire. Stitch the bunch on to the petal threads and twist the wire, stamens and thread to form a stalk.

4. Roll the fan to form a cone and secure at the base using enamelled wire.

5. Place the parts B around the cone and secure with enamelled wire.

6. Wrap floral tape around the stalk, concealing all wire and thread.

7. Place the leaves on the taped stalk and secure with enamelled wire. Conceal with more floral tape.

8. Shape the flowers and leaves and if necessary bend the stalk with the aid of pointed pliers.

Flower 2 – assembling

Flower

1. Lay the parts on top of each other slightly staggered, part A, B, C, D and finally E. Stitch the parts together in the middle.
2. Bend 2 floral stub wires in half. Form a hole with a darning needle and push the wires through the pre-formed hole.
3. Put a bunch of stamens through the middle.
4. Secure firmly with enamelled wire.
5. Wrap floral tape around the stalk

Leaf

6. Wrap floral tape around a piece of floral wire. Lay the wire behind the leaf and stitch to the middle rib.
7. Shape the flower and leaf.

Flower 3 – assembling

Bud

1. Bend a floral stub wire in half and push through a petal, Twist firmly together with the enamelled wire from the petal.
2. Place 3 stamens on the petal. Secure by twisting together with the enamelled wire.
3. Lay the other 2 petals around the stamens and first petal and secure firmly with enamelled wire.
4. Wrap floral tape around the wire and attach the leaves.

Flower

5. Form a bunch of 7-9 stamens and overlap the petals around the stamens. Secure firmly with enamelled wire.
6. Attach the flower to the lower part of the stalk.
7. Shape the flower and leaves.

Flower 4 – assembling

1. Stitch the parts C evenly spaced on top of part A.
2. Stitch on part B with running stitches and gather together in the middle.
3. Bend a floral stub wire in half and push through the flower. See photograph. Twist the wire firmly to form a stalk.
4. Sew a running thread along the inner side of part D.
5. Gather to form a rosette and stitch to the middle of the flower, concealing the wire.
6. Sew small beads in the middle.
7. Gently push up the upper petals and roll the parts C on a suitable knitting pin. Start at the point and roll in to form a spiral.
8. Wrap floral tape around the stalk.
9. Shape the flower and spirals.

Flower 5 – assembling

Flower

1. Place part B over part C, with part A on the top. Stitch firmly together.
2. Bend a floral stub wire in half and push it through the gathering point. Twist together with the enamelled wire.
3. Wrap floral tape around the stalk.
4. Stitch part D to form a cone and press the point tightly together. Stitch the cone to part E. See photograph.
5. Stitch the top edges of part E together to form the flower trumpet.
6. Stitch the trumpet on to the flower petals, concealing the wire.

Leaf

7. Wrap floral tape around a piece of floral wire. Lay the wire behind the leaf and stitch along the rib.
8. Shape the flower and leaves.

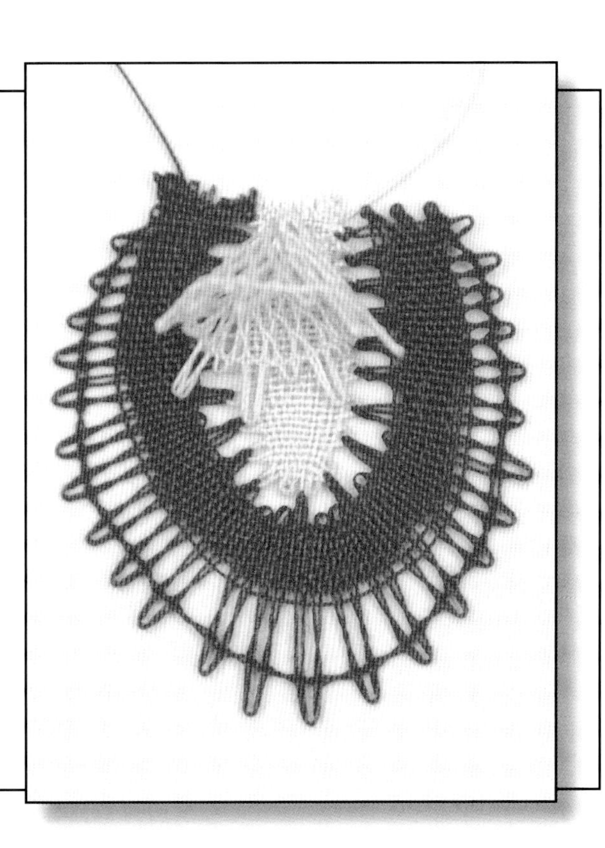

Flower 6 – assembling

1. Lay the inner petals slightly overlapping each other and stitch together at the base.
2. Place a stamen in the middle and stitch in place.
3. Bend a floral stub wire in half and push through the middle. Twist the wire to form a stalk.
4. Roll the petals to form a cone and secure with enamelled wire. See photograph.
5. Position the outer petals and secure again with enamelled wire.
6. Wrap floral tape around the stalk and position the leaves lower down the stalk.
7. Shape the flowers and leaves.

Flower 7 – assembling

1. Lay the parts B together in a star formation and stitch to form a large flower.
2. Bend a floral stub wire in half. Pre-prick a hole in the middle of the flower with a darning needle and push through the wire. Twist the wire firmly to form a stalk and wrap with floral tape.
3. Lay the parts C together in a star formation and stitch together to form a small flower.
4. Stitch the parts A to the small flower and sew beads in the middle.
5. Sew a running thread through all the lilac points. Pull together and tie a knot.
6. Remove the running thread when the lace has been given an extra stiffening.
7. Place a floral wire in the big leaf and twist together. Place the small leaves as a pair on the stalk.
8. Work several flowers and form a trail.

Flower 8 - assembling

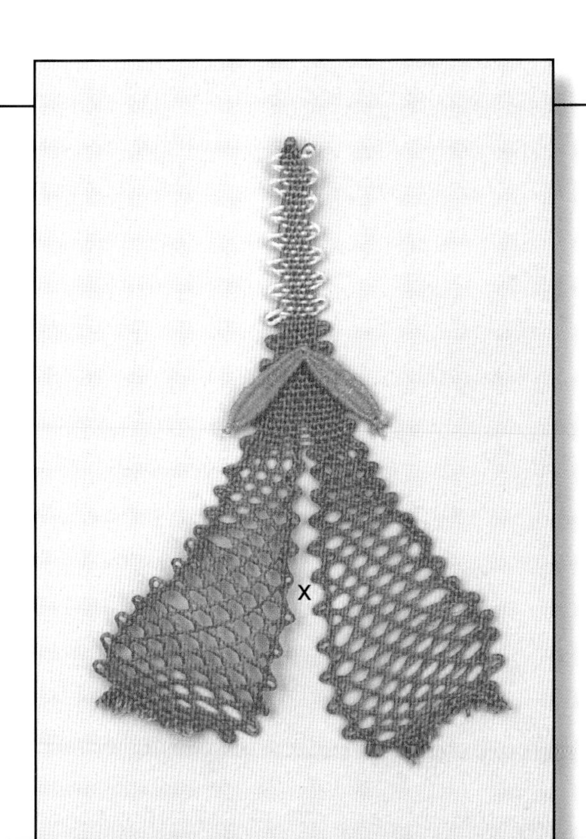

Flower
1. Place the parts B over part A and stitch together.
2. Place the parts C over A and B and stitch together.
3. Bend a floral stub wire in half and push through the middle of the petals.
4. Twist the wire firmly together with the enamelled wire and form the stalk. Wrap with floral tape.
5. Stitch part E to part D. See photograph. Sew the split parts together from x up to the middle.
6. Stitch part D to the middle of the flower concealing the wire.
7. Roll the point of part D over the middle of the flower and hold with a pin until the work has been given an extra stiffening. Remove the pin when the lace is dry.

Leaf
8. Wrap floral tape on a piece of floral wire and lay the wire behind the leaf. Stitch to the rib.
9. Shape the flower and leaves.

Flower 9 – assembling

1. Place the parts C over part A and stitch together.
2. Bend a floral stub wire in half and push through the flower centre. Twist firmly together with the enamelled wire to form a stalk.
3. Place the parts B on top of C and A and stitch together.
4. Place part D in the middle with the white point upwards. See phototgraph. Stitch in place to conceal the wire.
5. Roll the white point inwards and hold in place with a pin.
6. Fold the yellow points in towards the middle and hold in position with a pin.
7. Give the lace an extra stiffening and remove the pins when dry.
8. Position the leaves further down the stalk.
9. Shape the flower and leaves.

Flower 10 – assembling

1. Lay the 7 double tallies on top of each other and twist together in the middle with a piece of enamelled wire, forming a small bunch.
2. Surround with the parts A and secure with enamelled wire. See photograph.
3. Surround with parts B and secure with enamelled wire. Twist all the enamelled wires together to form a stalk and wrap with floral tape.
4. Form a stalk with floral stub wire and wrap with floral tape. Position the large leaf at the top followed by the 2 other leaves opposite each other. Position the flowers further down the stalk. Alternate the flowers and leaves.
5. Shape the flowers and leaves.

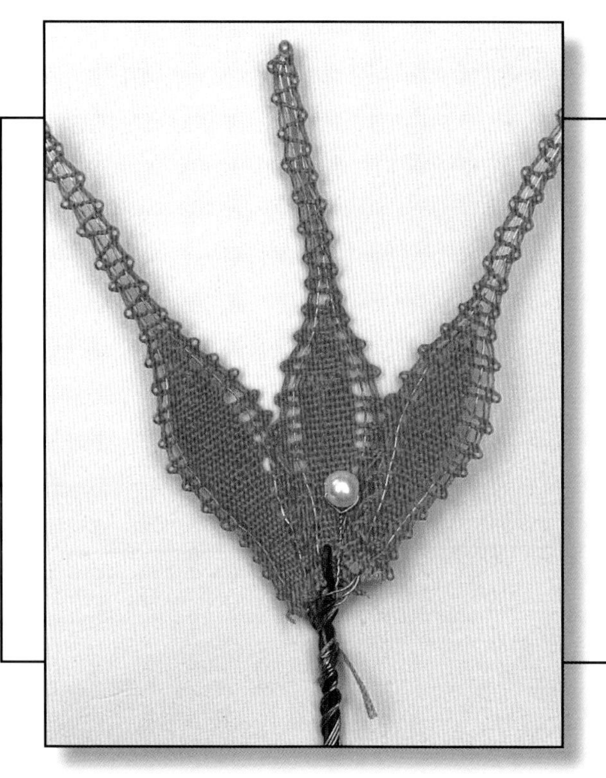

Flower 11 – assembling

1. Stitch the petals together at their base.
2. Thread a pearl on a piece of enamelled wire. Twist the wire firmly and stitch to the flower middle.
3. Bend a floral stub wire in half and push through the flower middle. Twist together with the enamelled wire to form a stalk. See photograph.
4. Sew the petals together to form a funnel. Secure with enamelled thread at the base and wrap floral tape around the stalk.
5. Position the flowers on the stalk with the leaves below (smaller leaves innermost).
6. Shape the flowers and leaves.

Flower 12 – Assembling

Stamens
1. Thread a bead on a 15cm piece of enamelled wire.
2. Bend in half and twist firmly together.
3. Form a bunch of ca. 9 stamens and secure with enamelled wire.

Flower
4. Surround the stamens with parts B and secure with enamelled wire.
5. Then position parts A and finally C. See photograph.
6. Twist all the enamelled wires to form a stalk.
7. Wrap floral tape around the stalk and shape the flowers.

Flower 13 – Assembling

Flower
1. Bend a floral stub wire in half and push through a petal, part A. Press together.
2. Form a bunch of ca.7 stamens, lay them on the petal and secure with enamelled wire.
3. Position the last 2 parts of part A on the first and secure with enamelled wire.
4. Add parts B and finally parts C in the gaps.
5. Twist the enamelled wires in with the stub wire to form a stalk and wrap with floral tape.

Bud
6. Lay a stamen on a petal, part D and secure with enamelled wire.
7. Position the other 2 parts of part D on the first and secure with enamelled wire.
8. Twist all the enamelled wires to form a stalk and wrap with floral tape.
9. Shape the flower, buds and leaves to form a bouquet.

Flower 14 – Assembling

1. Lay the parts A together with the petals off set. Hold together with paper clips. See photograph. Stitch together in the middle.
2. Repeat with parts B, which are then laid under parts A.
3. Sew a running thread around the middle, through all parts. Gather together and knot the thread at the back of the flower.
4. Bend a floral stub wire in half and push through the middle of the flower. Twist firmly to form a stalk.
5. Sew 7-9 beads in the middle of the flower.
6. Wrap floral tape around the stalk and shape the flower.

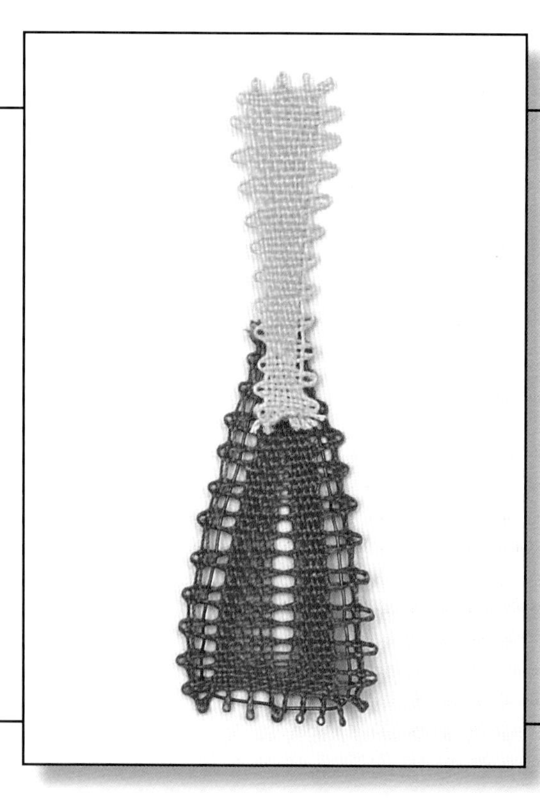

Flower 15 – Assembling

1. Lay parts C over each other and stitch together at their base.
2. Bend a floral stub wire in half and push through the flower middle. Twist firmly together with the enamelled wires to form a stalk.
3. Wrap floral tape around the stalk.
4. Lay the yellow part C on part B. See photograph.
5. Sew together and stitch on to the flower concealing the wire.
6. Roll the yellow part downwards forming a fruit bud.
7. Place a pin in the fruit bud to hold in position and give the lace an extra stiffening. Remove the pin when dry.
8. Shape the flower.

Flower 16 – Assembling

Bud
1. Stagger the parts D together and secure with enamelled wire at their base.
2. Bend a floral stub wire in half and push through the base of the bud. Twist firmly together with the enamelled wires from the petals to form a stalk. Wrap with floral tape.
3. Run a thread through the petal tips to keep the bud closed.

Flower
4. Form a bunch with parts B and secure with enamelled wire.
5. Position the small petals in the gaps. See photograph. Position the parts A outermost.
6. Twist all the enamelled wires to form a stalk and wrap with floral tape.
7. Position the flower and bud on the stalk and place the leaves lower down.
8. Shape the flower and leaves.

Flower 17 – Assembling

Flower
1. Place part B on part A with the petals off set. Stitch together in the middle.
2. Bend a floral stub wire in half and push diagonally through the flower. See photograph.
3. Form a bunch of ca. 15 stamens. Place on the parts C and secure firmly with enamelled wire.
4. Put the stamens through the middle of the flower. Press together with the floral wire.
5. Secure firmly with enamelled wire on the underside of the flower and wrap floral tape around the stalk.

Leaf
6. Bend a floral stub wire in half and push through the base of a leaf. Twist firmly together with the enamelled wire. Wrap floral wire on the stalk and position the other leaves on the stalk.
7. Shape the flower and leaves.

Flower 18 – Assembling

Bud

1. Stitch 2 petals together at the sides.
2. Bend a floral stub wire in half and push through the base of the bud. Twist firmly together with the enamelled wires to form a stalk.
3. Stitch the on last petal to close the bud.
4. Wrap floral tape around the stalk.

Flower

5. Place part B on part A and stitch together.
6. Stitch part C over A and B.
7. Bend a floral stub wire in half and push through the middle of the flower.
8. Twist the wire firmly together with the enamelled wires to form a stalk. Wrap with floral tape.
9. Stitch part D and the 2 parts of part F to the middle of the flower, with the threads pointing towards the middle. See photograph.
10. Fold the enamelled wire of part E behind the flower. Cut the ends with ca. 1cm tail. Stitch to the middle of the flower. Fold the fruit bud down over the sewing and hold in position with a pin.
11. Give the lace an extra stiffening.

Branch

12. Place 2 buds at the top of the branch. Position the flowers further down the branch and place the leaves in pairs in between. Place the larger leaf lowest.

Comparison Chart

If it is difficult to find the recommended threads, DMC Mouliné 25 can be substituted in the same colour. The corresponding DMC Mouliné 25 art. 117 thread is given for the Mayflower, Anchor and Venus threads used in this book.
Work with 1 of the 6 strands.

Anchor col 46, red	DMC col 666, red
Anchor col 249, yellow	DMC col 743, yellow
Anchor col 97, lilla	DMC col 553, lilac
Anchor col 259, gentle green	DMC col 772, gentle green
Anchor col 107, lilac	DMC col 327, lilac
Anchor col 01, white	DMC col B5200, white
Anchor col 756, light yellow	DMC col 745, light yellow
Anchor col 108 light lilac	DMC col.155, light lilac
Mayflower col 1120, orange	DMC col 741, orange
Mayflower col 5520, light green	DMC col. 470, light green
Mayflower col 2110, green	DMC col 895, grøn
Mayflower col 1438, yellow	DMC col 741, yellow
Venus col 675, liac	DMC col 3837 lilac
Venus col EM-500, dark lilac	DMC col 550 dark lilac
Venus col 195 red/brown	DMC col 3857 red/brown

Suppliers List

Threads, enamelled wire, floral stub wire, floral tape, stiffener and beads:

"Smykke – Sten og Knipleboden"
Tlf. +45 56 78 82 23
email: info@kniplinger.dk
www.kniplinger.dk

Metal wires
www.wires.co.uk (enamelled wire)
www.angelo-decoration.com (lackdraht)

Stamens and beads:

"Hobby og Mini"
Tlf. +45 59 29 22 25